This is the stuff yo ̶u̶ ̶h̶a̶v̶e̶ ̶b̶e̶e̶n̶ embarrassed to ask about the world of modern business.

The *What You Need to Know …* books can get you up to speed on a core business subject fast. Whether it's for a new job, a new responsibility, or a meeting with someone you need to impress, these books will give you what you need to get by as someone who knows what they're talking about.

Each book contains:

- ▶ **What It's all About** – a summary of key points
- ▶ **Who You Need to Know** – the basics about the key players
- ▶ **Who Said It** – quotes from key figures
- ▶ **How You Need to Do it** – key steps to put your new-found knowledge into practice
- ▶ **What You Need to Read** – books and online resources if you want to deepen your knowledge
- ▶ **If You Only Remember One Thing** – a one-liner of the most important information

You might also want to know:

- ▶ *What You Need to Know about Business*
- ▶ *What You Need to Know about Economics*
- ▶ *What You Need to Know about Strategy*
- ▶ *What You Need to Know about Leadership*
- ▶ *What You Need to Know about Marketing*

WHAT YOU NEED TO KNOW ABOUT PROJECT MANAGEMENT

FERGUS O'CONNELL

CAPSTONE

This edition first published 2011
© 2011 Fergus O'Connell

Registered office
Capstone Publishing Ltd. (A Wiley Company), The Atrium, Southern Gate, Chichester, West Sussex, PO19 8SQ, United Kingdom

For details of our global editorial offices, for customer services and for information about how to apply for permission to reuse the copyright material in this book please see our website at www.wiley.com.

Wiley also publishes its books in a variety of electronic formats. Some content that appears in print may not be available in electronic books.

Designations used by companies to distinguish their products are often claimed as trademarks. All brand names and product names used in this book are trade names, service marks, trademarks or registered trademarks of their respective owners. The publisher is not associated with any product or vendor mentioned in this book. This publication is designed to provide accurate and authoritative information in regard to the subject matter covered. It is sold on the understanding that the publisher is not engaged in rendering professional services. If professional advice or other expert assistance is required, the services of a competent professional should be sought.

Library of Congress Cataloguing-in-Publication Data

9780857081315 (paperback), 9780857081469 (ebook), 9780857081605 (epub), 9780857081612 (emobi)

A catalogue record for this book is available from the British Library.

Set in 10.5pt New Baskerville by Toppan Best-set Premedia Limited

For Davida Irene Hulse

CONTENTS

INTRODUCTION

This book will be of immense value to you if any of the following six situations apply to you:

One. You're new to project management. It will tell you exactly what you have to do to plan, execute and bring a project to a successful conclusion.

Two. Your boss has just called you into his office, handed you a pile of stuff and told you that you're going to be leading the Poison Chalice project. Oh, and by the way, it's got to be done by the end of year, and the budget's already been fixed and you can't hire any more people. This book will tell you what to do (and what not to do) next. It will you show that – depending on what your next move is – you could actually consign the project to disaster there and then.

Three. You're tired of fire fighting/late hours/nasty surprises and would like to find a better way to get your work done.

Four. You've ever been handed what appears to be (or definitely is) an impossible project.

Five. You're an experienced project manager. The book is a full-bodied refresher and checklist of the key things required to make a project successful. It will remind you of these key things, some of which you may have either forgotten or not realised the full significance of.

And finally – six – have you ever had this happen to you? Somebody comes running in to you and says, 'This should only take an hour or two' and two years later you're still working on it. If you have then this book is for you.

The book covers everything you need to know about project management in eight chapters called:

Chapter 1 – Goal Setting
Chapter 2 – Estimating
Chapter 3 – Supply and Demand
Chapter 4 – Managing Risk
Chapter 5 – Managing Expectations
Chapter 6 – Tracking and Status Reporting
Chapter 7 – Running Multiple Projects
Chapter 8 – Having a Life.

The first six chapters take you through everything you need to know to run a project from start to finish. They can (and should) be read sequentially as they take you, step-by-step, through what you need to do. Once you have these six chapters under your belt, Chapter 7 builds on that knowledge by telling you how to run more than one project at the same time. Finally, there seems to be a view in the world that project managers are people who should just work all the hours God sends to get projects done. Chapter 8 shows you how you can be a successful project manager and still have a life.

Each chapter has a number of common elements. The guts of each chapter explain exactly what you have to do and why you have to do it. Then there are some other dead useful things:

▶ **What It's All About** – A quick summary at the start of each chapter listing the key messages that will be covered.

▶ **Who You Need to Know** – Key figures you need to know in project management. These will either be people who have shaped the discipline of project management or are/were great project managers from whom you can learn.

▶ **Who Said It** – Quotes from famous figures to remind, inspire and amuse you.

▶ **How to Do It** – Key practical tips for using the knowledge in each chapter. These boxes will describe the tools and techniques that you need to use and give examples of their use.

▶ **What You Need to Read** – Suggestions of 3-5 key sources for further reading

▶ **If You Only Remember One Thing** – Lines summing up the contents of each chapter at the end of each chapter.

Since the book is going to spend a lot of time talking about projects, perhaps this is a good place to define what a project is. There are also a couple of related terms – 'programme' and 'programme management' – which need to be referred to as well.

The Project Management Institute's (PMI's) *Project Management Body of Knowledge* (PMBOK) give definitions of the words 'project' and 'project management'. You don't need to worry too much about these here. These definitions lay great stress on the fact that a project is different from business-as-usual type things like doing the end of month accounts or processing customer requests.

But it's been my experience that *anything* can be a project. Large or small, with a cast of thousands or just you, in work or outside of it – anything can be treated as a project and the things covered in this book can be successfully applied to it. In your project management travels, you'll also come across the phrase 'programme management'. What's a programme? It's just a big project or you can also think of it as a group of related projects being done together. Programme management, then, is the management of such a beast.

So:

▶ Anything can be a project.
▶ A task is just a small project. A project is just a big task.
▶ A programme is just a series of projects. For example, the 2012 Olympic Games is a programme. However, the 2012 Games is also just a big project – or indeed, a big task.

Project management, then, is making your project happen. It's the planning (and, in particular, the estimating) of the project and then, the execution of the plan to bring the project to a successful conclusion. Thus, project management can be applied to anything.

While this definition may sound loose to you, it has the huge advantage that the skills you're going to learn in this book are widely applicable to a vast (in fact, infinite) range of problems and situations.

Good project management is less about how to draw a Gantt Chart or wondering what 'Critical Path' means, and more about *behaviour*. There are certain behaviours that lead to good project management and certain behaviours that are guaranteed to drive you onto the rocks. This book tells you what those good behaviours are. But – more importantly – it will motivate you into adopting these good behaviours.

Behaviour change is hard. You know it yourself. If you've ever tried to give up smoking, go on a diet, take up running or whatever – it's tough. It's tough and it's easy to slide back into your old ways. For nearly twenty years I have been teaching courses (www. etpint.com) on how to adopt these good behaviours. This book incorporates everything I have learned during that time.

If you do the things that this book describes then:

> ▶ All your projects will work out successfully.
> ▶ Your projects will get done as quickly and as cheaply as possible.
> ▶ Your projects will get done with far less fire fighting and unpleasant surprises, thereby saving and freeing up much valuable time.
> ▶ You will be able to make commitments on project budgets and delivery dates with maximum confidence – and deliver on these commitments.
> ▶ You will build a track record of consistent project delivery.
> ▶ You'll be able to have a life.

If all of this appeals to you then turn the page and let's get started.

CHAPTER 1

GOAL SETTING

WHAT IT'S ALL ABOUT

- ▶ The big problem in project management
- ▶ The magic line – what to say when you get handed a project and what *not* to say
- ▶ Setting a clear goal.
- ▶ Controlling changes to the goal
- ▶ Maximising the win-conditions of the stakeholders
- ▶ The definition of a successful project
- ▶ The way to set SMART goals
- ▶ When to consider something a project

THE BIG PROBLEM IN PROJECT MANAGEMENT

Why is it that so many projects that we see, read about or get involved in, go wrong? In my experience, the number one reason for this is that they were never actually possible in the first place. You see, project management is actually the most difficult job in the world. This is because in project management, we get asked to make a prediction of the future (a plan) and then make the prediction come true (execute the plan). If you could actually do that each time, you probably wouldn't be reading this book. Indeed I probably wouldn't have written it. Instead I'd be spending my time at the race track or in casinos or buying lottery tickets – if I could predict the future and have it come true.

If that wasn't bad enough, we often get asked to make these predictions in a very strange way. Imagine if your car was acting up. You take it to the garage and say: 'I don't know what's wrong with my car, but I need you to fix it in the next half hour and I'll give you fifty pounds/euros/dollars for it.' It would be a strange thing to say. But imagine the mechanic in the garage simply responded with 'sure'. That would surely be much stranger. And half an hour later, as you drive your car out of the forecourt having given him the fifty pounds, you'd be wondering what he'd done to your car and whether he had, in fact, done anything. Of course, we couldn't imagine such a silly scenario in a garage.

However, in a lot of the projects that we get handed, such conversations are almost routine. Somebody says, 'Here's the project. I don't know much about it. But it's got to be done by this date for this budget. You can't hire any more people and good luck with that.'

It's important to realise that when you're given a project, you're actually given two things. There is the project itself, for example the 2012 Olympic Games, and then there are the constraints. Constraints are things like:

- ▶ it has to be done by a certain date;
- ▶ or within a certain budget;
- ▶ or with certain resources;
- ▶ or the scope of the project has already been decided;
- ▶ or some combination of these.

If you try to deal with the project and the constraints together, you're potentially going to get yourself into a lot of trouble. Because as you think about the project, you think about all the stuff you're going to have to do and all the time that's going to take. But the constraints are telling you that you're not going to be given that time. And you're probably thinking that you are going to need four, five, possibly six people to do this project. Other constraints are telling you that you'll lucky to get a man and a dog to work on it.

This book will talk about the reasons why projects fail. As I've already said, the number one reason that they fail is that they were never actually possible in the first place. Somebody said, 'Here's the project and here are the constraints' and everybody said, 'Sure'. So the first thing you need to know when you get handed a project is the Magic Line.

THE MAGIC LINE

When somebody hands you a project, the last thing on earth you should say is 'sure'. Instead you need to say, '**I'll take a look at it.**' Somebody comes running in to you and says here it is and they need an answer right now. You say, 'I'll take a look at it'. Somebody's at a meeting, jumping up and down, banging the table and saying, 'I need to know *now*'. You say, 'I'll take a look at it. Let's take a time out so that I can do that.' Somebody says, 'The greatest of all bosses needs an answer by four o'clock today.' You say, 'I'm going to have to take a look at it.'

It's the only reasonable and sensible answer when you're given a project.

And in a million other normal trades, industries and professions, this is exactly what happens. Because when you *do* take your car to the garage and say, 'I don't know what's wrong with my car ...', they don't say 'sure'. They say, 'I'll take a look at it.' And the guy does exactly that. He lifts the bonnet or pokes around under the car and then tells you what's possible and what's not possible. You may be waving your 50 euros but if they say to you, 'Listen mate, you've got three choices. You can get a reconditioned engine, you can get a new engine, or you can go and talk to sales about a new car', then you have some decisions to make.

This idea of an examination first to bring up the options, followed by a plan of action is standard in most normal trades, industries and professions. It's the right thing to do. It's also the right thing to do on projects.

WHO SAID IT

"If one does not know to which port one is sailing, no wind is favourable."
– Seneca

Once you've said, 'I'll take a look at it', it means that you can park the constraints while you try to understand what the project is all about. The first thing you have to do then is to figure out the goal of the project. There's nothing too surprising about that. There are three issues that you must address here and they're all big project killers if you don't get them right.

1. THE GOAL OF THE PROJECT MUST BE CLEAR AND NOT VAGUE

You must put a sort of boundary around the project. You then clarify that the things within the boundary are part of the project while the things outside the boundary are not. You may have heard of 'in scope' (within the boundary) and 'out of scope' (outside the boundary).

So:

▶ In scope: The project will do these things. It will bring these benefits. It will have these features. It will deliver these deliverables.

▶ Out of scope: The project will *not* do these things. They are parts of other projects or initiatives or systems. They're not part of your thing.

If you succeed in fixing this boundary, think of it like this – a box:

If you fail to fix this boundary then it would be drawn like this – a cloud:

The problem with projects whose goal is 'cloudy' is that they can't finish. They can't finish because they don't know what 'finish' is. With the clear (boxed) goal, it's almost like the items within the box form a checklist. When all of these things are done, then the project is done. With the cloud we can't say that and then what will happen is the following.

This is what the team will deliver:

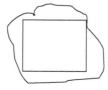

But the boss will say, 'This is what I was expecting.'

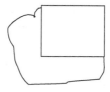

And the customer will say, 'I thought we were getting this.'

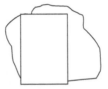

And the resulting gaps in expectations will cause a lot of unhappiness to a lot of people.

We don't have to look too far to find projects where this has been a problem. There was the movie *Waterworld* which had an initial budget of $100 million and ended up costing twice that. This was a film where they were rewriting the script (the definition of the goal of the project) while they were shooting the film. Or take the London Stock Exchange's (in)famous TAURUS project which has become a classic case study in project failure.

TAURUS (Transfer and Automated Registration of Uncertificated Stock) was an IT project at the LSE designed to result in paperless trading and computerised shareholding. The main aim of Taurus was to reduce costs and the time taken to process share transactions. The project was started in the mid 1980's and was finally scrapped in 1993 at a cost of about £800 million. The main reason for its failure was that the scope (goal) of the project was never fixed and so continued to expand over the life of the project.

After the project was cancelled and the recriminations began, one simple statement – from amongst a plethora issued by the Stock Exchange – told the story. 'We were testing parts of the system, while *other parts hadn't been designed or built*' [my italics]. A cloudy goal? You said it.

So, your goal has to be clear, not vague. We have to have boxes, not clouds.

2. YOU MUST CONTROL CHANGES TO THE GOAL

Let's say you succeed in boxing off your goal and then you start the project. What happens then? Well, what happens then is that changes start happening. Here's something they should have told you about but they didn't. Here's something you should have seen but you missed it. Here's a change in say, the business or the regulatory climate – something, for example, that your competitors have done that you're going to have to respond to.

And there's no problem with any of this – after all, the rate of change in the 21st century has become a cliché so we're going to have to get used to this – provided you control the changes that occur. You can't let them happen in an uncontrolled sort of way.

Because here's the next big mistake that project managers make. They assume that because they've committed to a plan/budget/schedule/deadline/resourcing for a certain project scope, i.e. a certain set of things in the box, these must remain unchanged even if scope changes. Here's a simple example to show that this is ridiculous.

Let's say that the project you're asked to do is to 'make a container for water'. After some discussions with the customer, you understand that what they want is a glass – cylindrical, made of glass, a certain height, diameter, etc. Okay, you start the project. Now it turns out, once the project gets rolling that that wasn't really what the customer wanted. They wanted a jug. A jug is also a container for water. But it's a more complicated piece of engineering than a glass. The plan/budget/schedule/deadline/resourcing to make a jug is not the plan/budget/schedule/deadline/resourcing to make a glass. And if you're not convinced of that, a swimming pool is also a container for water. The plan for a glass is not the plan for a swimming pool! But many project managers fall into the trap of thinking that since they committed to certain targets for the glass, they must deliver the swimming pool to the same targets. If you think of the glass and the swimming pool you can see how ridiculous this is.

So then we have to ask the question, 'How could project managers be so stupid?' 'How could usually intelligent and educated people do something so dumb?' The answer lies in the expression, 'the customer is always right'. And yes, the customer *is* always right. The people for whom we're doing the project can change their minds in any way they want. But every time they change their minds, there's a price associated with that. There's a price in terms of time, money, resources – and controlling the changes means that we tell them the price. Some prices may be trivial – maybe they want the glass two millimetres wider in diameter and we can say, 'yep, no problem.' But some prices aren't trivial. The price of 'we don't want a glass, we want a swimming pool' is not trivial. We have to tell them the change in price.

So when changes occur on the project, as they invariably will, you have to know what to do. You'll be able to deal with some changes yourself, without bothering the people for whom you're doing the project. But for some changes you'll absolutely have to go back to these people. You need to make the right choices here. You need to know when to do one and when to do the other.

CHANGE CONTROL – ANOTHER WAY TO LOOK AT IT

If a change occurs on your project – it can be a small change like 'Charlie's gone sick for the day' or a big change like 'we don't want a glass, we want a swimming pool' – then there are three (and only three) ways you can deal with that change:

Big change

The first is you can say that this is a big change. The fancy term is a 'change to the project's terms of reference' or a 'change control event'. Some changes are like that, where what we are now being asked to do is significantly different from what we were originally doing.

Use contingency

Now, of course, lots of changes are *not* big changes. They're little slip-ups. Because Charlie *does* go sick for the day, the server goes down, a supplier lets us down, or something simple turns out to be complicated – the thousand little things that are sent to try us. For these we need to have contingency in the plan. It's perhaps worth remembering the following. Think of it as the Project Manager's Prayer. It goes like this:

> 'Unexpected stuff happens on projects.
> Most of it is *bad* unexpected stuff.
> Sometimes I get a lucky break,
> But mostly, it is bad unexpected stuff.
> For this I need to have contingency in the plan.'

You do! You need to have contingency in your plan.

'Suck it up'

Finally then, if something is a big change, you might not have the guts to say that to the people for whom you're doing the project. And if there's no contingency in the plan, either because you never put it in, or you did, but then some genius took it out, then there's only one other possible way of dealing with changes. To put it bluntly – that is to suck it up! Suck it up means work nights, work weekends, bring work home with you, tell your significant others that you won't be home tonight or you can't take your holidays during the project and so on.

Let's be clear. There is nothing intrinsically wrong with sucking it up. If you accept the basic idea that project management is about predicting the future, then there may be times when you *do* have to suck it up – to hit a deadline, meet a milestone, solve a customer problem. No problem with that. But if sucking it up is the *only* thing you do when changes occur then that's a huge problem.

On a healthy project there may be times when you shout, 'Big change!', there may be times when you have to use your contingency, and then there may be times when you have to suck it up. No problem with that. That's a healthy project. An unhealthy project is where every change is dealt with by sucking it up. Most of us have experienced such projects. They're not fun.

WHO SAID IT

"Begin with the end in mind."
– Stephen Covey

3. YOU MUST MAXIMISE THE WIN-CONDITIONS OF THE STAKEHOLDERS

You've boxed off your goal. You now know that you must control changes, i.e. make the right choice from the three possibilities when changes occur. The third and final thing you must do when goal setting is to maximise the win-conditions of the stakeholders. It may sound like a terrible piece of management waffle, but it's actually a useful phrase.

The stakeholders are the people with a stake in the project. More specifically, they are the individuals or groups of people affected by the project. Individuals can be stakeholders – Fergus is a stakeholder, for example or Ellen is a stakeholder – or a group of people can be a stakeholder. For example, all of your organisation's customers could be a stakeholder or the body that regulates your industry could be a stakeholder. Generally speaking, some stakeholders are more important than others. You might, for example, see your boss as being a more important stakeholder than a supplier.

We tend to think of the obvious stakeholders – me, my team, my boss, the customer. But if we throw the net a bit wider, think a bit more carefully, we can come up with other stakeholders. There may be people in other departments of our organisation or people in other organisations. The test is – are they affected by the project? If they are in any way, whether positively or negatively, then they are a stakeholder in the project.

One particular stakeholder that you may come across is the one known as the 'project sponsor' – a term that is particularly popular in the UK. The project sponsor is generally a fairly senior person in the organisation who (a) sees a need for the project and (b) is responsible to the business for the success of it. In almost all cases, the project sponsor is *not* the project manager.

Also it's worth mentioning that there is no correlation between the size of the project and the number of stakeholders. Small projects can have a large number of stakeholders or vice versa. It just varies.

Each stakeholder then, has win-conditions. Win-conditions are what that particular stakeholder would regard as a successful outcome to the project. In general, different stakeholders have different win-conditions. Often win-conditions can be pulling in opposite directions. For example, if I'm the boss who has given the troops the impossible deadline, then maybe one of my win-conditions is that the troops hit the deadline. If, on the other hand, I'm a team member who has been working burnout hours for the last twelve months, then maybe my win-condition is that I just want to work a forty-hour week. Also since some stakeholders are more important than others, we will tend to treat some win-conditions as being more important than others.

Finally then, maximising the win-conditions of the stakeholders means, given that we have all these different win-conditions, being able to come up with a combined or composite set of win-conditions that will keep everybody happy. This is what leads to a successful project.

THE DEFINITION OF A SUCCESSFUL PROJECT?

So what's a successful project? Quite simply, a successful project is one that results in happy stakeholders. You tell the stakeholders what they're going to get from the project and that's what they get. When you put it like that it sounds pretty simple. When you put it as 'predict the future and have it come true', you see what a tall order it really is.

24

But this is what the stakeholders want. So obviously then, if you want to deliver happy stakeholders, the first question is, 'What's going to make them happy?' You have to find out. And how do you do that? Go and ask them. Don't assume that you know. Or, by all means, take a shot at it yourself first, but then go and confirm it with them. And get them to sign something or confirm in writing.

This is goal setting. It's the single most important thing you'll do in your project. Finding out who the people affected by the project are, and what they hope to get from it is essential if you're to have any chance of your project succeeding.

SMART GOALS

Here's another useful thing to bear in mind when you're identifying the goal of your project. You need to think in terms of your goal being SMART:

> ▶ **S**pecific – The goal is precise, not vague. 'Learn a musical instrument' is vague, 'learn to play the guitar' is precise.
>
> ▶ **M**easurable – A goal can be measured whether it has been achieved or not. The goal, 'learn to play the guitar' cannot really be measured; the goal 'have played my first gig before a live audience and be paid for it' can.

25

▶ **A**chievable – The goal is attainable as opposed to some pie-in-the-sky nonsense. If the goal you had set yourself was, for example, 'to practice the guitar three hours a day, every day' but you had a full-time job, a family and were renovating a house, then this goal is probably not achievable. The goal, 'practice an hour each evening' might be.

▶ **R**ealistic – The goal actually makes sense. The goal 'become as a good a guitar player as John Williams in one year' makes no sense; 'play a gig in front of an audience within one year' (maybe) does.

▶ **T**ime-bound – The goal has a timeframe – essentially a deadline. The goal, 'play a gig in front of an audience' is not time-bound; the goal 'play a gig in front of an audience within one year' is.

WHO SAID IT

"Those last few seconds seemed never-ending. The faint line of the finishing tape stood ahead as a haven of peace, after the struggle … If I faltered, there would be no arms to hold me and the world would be a cold, forbidding place."
– **Roger Bannister**

GOAL SETTING GIVES YOU THE MOTIVATION TO DO THE PROJECT

In some ways, the most important thing about goal setting is that it provides you with the motivation to get the project done. You paint the picture of what life will be like when the project is over. As it becomes clearer in your mind, the sense of how you will feel when the project is done, begins to take root. If you can communicate this to your team it becomes the motivation that takes all of you forward. There will almost invariably be tough times ahead. The picture of the goal – the 'vision', if you like – will help to sustain you during those dark days.

WHEN TO CONSIDER SOMETHING A PROJECT

The final question to ask when it comes to goal setting is *when* does it apply? Or another way of asking the question is, how big does something have to be before you should treat it as a project?

If you've ever had the experience of somebody saying, 'this shouldn't take you very long', or 'would you mind doing this quick thing?' – and two years later you're still working on it because it turned out to be bigger than the Aswan Dam, then you should consider doing this on every request that comes your way.

Say, 'I'll take a look at it' and then go figure out the goal of the project, which is described shortly in the *How You Need To Do It* section. Then, if it is truly a small thing, great. More often than not though, you'll have found complications that you would have missed had you not done the simple goal setting that we're going to describe. You'll also have saved yourself some very deep pain, which, you have to agree, is a very good thing indeed.

WHO YOU NEED TO KNOW
The World's First Project Manager

The truth is that we don't know. The man (or woman) who project managed the Great Pyramid, is a contender. Built around 2560 BC, it is still a matter of conjecture how the large square stones of which it is made were lifted into place. But then you've got something like Stonehenge which – it is believed – was built six hundred years earlier, around 3100 BC.

The world's first project manager was probably one of our caveman ancestors who, one day with his colleagues, decided that with winter coming they needed to go and bag themselves a woolly mammoth. (We're talking somewhere around 150,000 years ago.) Sitting around the fire one evening they built their plan. The project manager had gathered the team together. (Always a good move – involve the team in the planning.) They would have to have weapons, they decided – clubs, spears, that kind of thing. And then having found the woolly mammoth, some of them would have to drive it towards where the rest of them would be waiting to kill it – maybe in some kind of canyon or dead end. Or they could dig a hole, somebody suggested. Cover it with leaves and sticks and have the woolly mammoth fall in. Good stuff – evaluate alternative ways the project could be done. Finally, perhaps they settled on the hole-with-sticks-and-leaves option.

Next morning they headed off, located a herd of woolly mammoth, found a suitable spot nearby and dug their hole. The hole was duly disguised and they went off to drive the mammoth towards the trap. A mammoth obligingly fell in and they killed it with their spears and clubs. Ah, but then a problem. In fact, two problems. How do we get nine tons of mammoth out of the hole? And how do we get that much meat, fur and bones back to the cave?

And so the world's first project cock-up took place: Failing to specify the correct goal of the project – in this case, 'get a supply of food for the winter' rather than 'kill the woolly mammoth' – continues to be one of the world's biggest project killers.

HOW YOU NEED TO DO IT
Establishing the Goal of Your Project

To establish the goal of your project, do the following:

1. Say 'I'll take a look at it.'
2. Park the constraints.
3. Answer the question 'how will I know when this project is over?' What point in time marks the end of this project? What is the final event that marks its conclusion? This will tell you the goal of the project.
4. Make a list of all the stakeholders. For each stakeholder, write down their 'win conditions' i.e. write down what they would regard as a successful project.
5. Some organisations have documents that they use to initiate projects. Two of the most common names for these documents are 'Project Charter' or 'Project Initiation Document'. Doing these steps will give you all the essential information you need to write one of these documents.

Example

Imagine your boss asks you to 'run a job advertisement' for a particular kind of person. She says it needs to be done by the end of the month [constraint].

When is this project over? Not the trivial question it might first appear. Often project goals are phrased very loosely. Is this project over when the advert runs in the paper, or when you get CVs in response to the ad, or when you interview some people, or when you hire somebody or what? All these are potentially valid endings to this project. You need to clarify this with your boss. Say it turns out to be just running the ad.

So the stakeholders and their win conditions would be defined as:

Stakeholder	Win conditions
Us	Run ad that reflects well on the company and doesn't upset anybody. It also should communicate why the jobs on offer are so attractive that you'd want to be mad not to apply.
Our boss	The ad sends out a positive message about the company.

Stakeholder	Win conditions
Existing employees	Doesn't upset anybody – uses only material that is in the public domain. Sends out a message that the company is one that people want to work for.
Potential employees	Sends out a message that the company is one that people want to work for.
Our customers	Sends out a message that the company is expanding, and is a good company to do business with.

So now you know all the key information about this project. You know who the stakeholders are, what's going to make them happy, what lies within the scope of the project and what will be regarded as the end of the project.

WHO SAID IT

"If you don't know where you're going,
you'll wind up somewhere else."
– Lawrence Peter 'Yogi' Berra

WHAT YOU NEED TO READ

▶ The Project Management Institute or PMI
(*www.pmi.org*) is the number one organisation
in the world for people involved in project
management. The website offers templates
for Project Charters and Project Initiation
Documents in the *Practical Guide to Project
Documentation*.

▶ The Association for Project Management, or
APM (*www.apm.org.uk*) is a UK-based organisation whose mission is 'to develop and promote
the professional disciplines of project and programme management for the public benefit'.

▶ *The Mythical Man Month and Other Essays on Software Engineering* by Frederick P. Brookes (Addison Wesley, 1995) is one of the classics of project management. Although it was written more than 20 years ago, many of the lessons in it are as valid now as they were then.

▶ As a novel, *The Deadline: A Novel About Project Management* by Tom DeMarco (Dorset House Publishing, 1997) is *terrible*. As a text on project management, it gives powerful lessons and insights.

▶ *Scott and Amundsen: Last Place on Earth* by Roland Huntford (Abacus, 2000) might sound like a strange choice, but even if you're not interested in travel or exploration, get your hands on it anyway. It's not often that we get to see the same project done by two different teams, with two spectacularly different outcomes.

IF YOU ONLY REMEMBER ONE THING

The only sensible answer when somebody hands you a project and a deadline is to say, 'I'll take a look at it.'

CHAPTER 2
ESTIMATING

WHAT IT'S ALL ABOUT

- ▶ Why you need to have a plan
- ▶ How to predict the future
- ▶ How to use previous projects when estimating
- ▶ The way to estimate duration and work
- ▶ Working out how much project management the project needs
- ▶ Project management methodologies
- ▶ Project management tools

NOW THAT YOU HAVE A GOAL, YOU HAVE TO HAVE A PLAN

Having established the goal of your project, the next thing you have to do is build a plan. A plan is a description of what you intend to do in the days, weeks and months ahead. In other words, it's a prediction of the future. Given that none of us can actually do this, then how are you to have any chance of success? Read on.

WHO SAID IT

"A goal without a plan is just a wish."
– Antoine de Saint-Exupery

HOW TO PREDICT THE FUTURE

Here's an exercise for you. There's a task in a project called 'Review document'. A bunch of people are

WHO YOU NEED TO KNOW
Vitruvius

Marcus Vitruvius Pollio was a Roman architect, engineer and author of *De Architectura*, a ten volume work on Roman architecture and engineering methods. In mentioning him, the book is really acknowledging any one of thousands of unknown Romans who designed, project managed and built aqueducts, temples, walls, public buildings, houses, towns, roads, cities, arenas during the time of the Roman Republic and subsequently, the Roman Empire. (And in picking the Romans, we should also acknowledge lots of other ancient civilisations where equivalent men (almost always) built equally spectacular buildings and edifices.)

To take just one example of the Roman's project management ability, you should – if you ever get the chance – visit the Pont du Gard near Nimes in France. The Pont du Gard was part of a 50 kilometre aqueduct bringing water to the Roman city of Nemausus (modern day Nimes). The gradient in the aqueduct i.e. the amount it fell over its 50 kilometre length was just 12 metres – a gradient of 1 in 4,000. (Yes, read that again – it's not a typo.) Oh, and just for good measure, the Pont du Gard was built nearly two thousand years ago and was constructed entirely without mortar. The stones of which it is made, some of which weigh six tons, were precisely cut to fit together and so, obviate the need for mortar. Good huh?

asked to come up with a time estimate for this task. How would *you* do this? Well, you might ask questions like:

- ▶ How big is the document?
- ▶ How many people are reviewing it?
- ▶ What kind of review is it?
- ▶ What do you mean by 'review'? For example, is it just one person's review of it? Or a bunch of people reviewing it?
- ▶ Does this task cover just the review itself or does it also include any updates to the document?

▶ Is it a second review? Or in fact, does 'review document' means several review and update cycles?

Once you know the answers to these questions – answers that give you more detail about the task – then you might then feel better able to give a time estimate.

And what would be the result? Well, it's highly likely that, if a bunch of people did this, there could be a factor of anything up to 100 between the highest and the lowest estimate!

What does this mean? Does it mean that you are not a very good estimator and that you should really consider doing something else beside project management? No. Not at all. What it means is that predicting the future is very difficult and you will never get it a hundred percent right. The best you can hope for is that you will be able to keep the error as small as possible. Detail is one of the keys to doing this.

The other key is to look at what happened on previous projects, and to ask the killer question: 'The last X times we carried out this task on projects, how long did it take?'

Looking at what happened on previous projects and having plenty of detail in the plan are the two things you need to do to keep the error in your estimation as small as possible i.e. to do good estimating.

1 Looking at What Happened on Previous Projects

In a perfect world, in your organisation, there would be records somewhere of all of the projects that were ever run. Then, when somebody had to run a new project, they could simply consult these records and learn from what had been done previously.

In most organisations such records either don't exist at all or are very incomplete, if they do. But don't worry, in chapter 6 you'll see how you can start to build these records for yourself. You'll also see why nothing will be more valuable to you in terms of improving your estimating ability – not to mention your ability to 'sell' your plan to your stakeholders.

WHO SAID IT

"The devil is in the detail."
– variously attributed to French writer
Gustave Flaubert, Michelangelo and others

2 Detail in the Plan

If you think about it, when anything gets done, it gets done through a sequence of events. Whether it's something as simple as cooking dinner or something vast like the 2010 World Cup, a sequence of jobs gets built. Somebody does something and then somebody does something else and so on until the thing is done. If you're the project manager running the project it is your job to build this sequence of events; to cause this chaining of jobs together to happen. It is these events which constitute the detail that must go into your plan. There are three ways this detail can be built into the plan. However, two of them are no good and only one of them makes any sense. Unfortunately, it's the two that are no good that tend to be the most widely used!

The first way that you can build the detailed sequence of events is not do anything at all – you just let fate or luck do it! Here's what working on such a project would be like. Charlie arrives at the office in the morning and says, 'Hmmm, what'll I do today?' He does something. Then he realises he needs something from somebody else, so he wanders down the corridor and says, 'Hey Fred, do you have that other thing?' But maybe Fred says he won't have that until Friday and so Charlie shrugs and does something else and so the project unfolds with things just … well, sort of happening.

Now clearly nobody would consciously do this and deliberately decide that they're going to let luck run their project. But in your organisation today there are almost certainly projects that are being run exactly like this. Typically, they're not being run like this because people are stupid or incompetent. They're being run like this because people don't have enough *time* available to run the project. If people are too busy, are trying to keep too many balls in the air, are multi-tasking so much that they don't have time available to run the project, then fate/luck just takes over. But you need to remember that fate/luck is the worst project manager there is.

The second way you can build the sequence of events is to do it in real time. Here's what this is like. You arrive at the office in the morning and look at your to-do list. You start doing the first thing on the list but then somebody reminds you to come to the nine-thirty meeting. During the meeting, somebody knocks on the door and says, 'Can I speak to you for a minute?' While you're speaking to them, your mobile phone rings so you answer that. Then your computer goes 'bing!' because an email has arrived. And then your land line rings … You get the idea. You sort of ricochet through the day. Gotta go here, gotta go there, do that thing, talk to that guy … You may be familiar with the 'f' word – 'fire fighting'.

Fire fighting is a term used to describe how you deal with crises or unexpected events. A fire fight occurs when something you didn't anticipate occurs and you have to deal with it.

Sure, fire fighting happens on projects. No matter how carefully they're planned, fire fights are going to happen. But not everything that happens on a project is a fire fight. Many things that happen on projects could have been predicted – if only you'd thought about them. Fire fighting – the recipe for a short, unhappy life – is certainly not the way to run a project.

That leaves one other possibility when it comes to building the sequence of events. This is to do it right at the beginning – before you have made any commitments to any stakeholders, before you start hiring people or allocating jobs or burning up the budget – you should build as much of the sequence of events as you can. Fire fights will still happen – but then you can save your energy for the things that are genuine fire fights; as opposed to the things which would never have become fire fights if only you had thought about them.

DURATION AND WORK

There are a couple of other essentials that need to be covered before getting into the business of estimating. The first of these is the difference between two quantities known as 'Duration' and 'Work'. Pay close attention. This is very important.

Duration, sometimes also called elapsed time, is *how long* something is going to take. It is measured in the normal units of time – hours, days, months and so on. The usual duration of a soccer match, for example, is 90 minutes. Durations are important because they enable you to figure out how long a particular job, or an entire project, is going to take. If you estimate the durations of all of the individual jobs in a project; then show which jobs depend on which other jobs, you can figure out the duration of the project.

But if you want to know how big a project is, or how many people you're going to need to get it done, or what it's going to cost, then duration isn't going to help you.

What you need in this case is something called work (sometimes also called 'effort'). This is simply how much stuff has to be done. Work is measured in units like man-days, person-hours, person-years and so on. The work in a soccer match, for example, if you count two teams of 11, a referee, two linesmen and a fourth official is 26 times 90 minutes i.e. 2,340 person-minutes which (divide by 60) gives 39 person-hours.

Sometimes there is a link between duration and work – as there was in the soccer match example we've just used – and sometimes there's no link. An example of there being no link is when we say, give somebody a document to review and give them say, a week to do it. There might be a person-hour's work in doing the review, but the duration is a week.

Finally, notice how work (and not duration) can enable you to work out the budget. If you know somebody's hourly or daily rate i.e. the price per person-hour or person-day, then you can figure out what a particular job is going to cost. Let's look at a little more at budgets.

THE BUDGET

Here's all you need to know. Each job in your plan will have a cost associated with it. This cost can come about in one of three ways:

▶ Labour only – The cost of this job is the work (in say, person-hours or person-days) multiplied by the hourly or daily rate, as appropriate. Where can you get this hourly or daily rate from? Go ask the Finance people. If they can't give it to you, make some kind of assumption. A common assumption would be to say that daily rate should be two to three times daily salary. (There is more about assumptions in a little while.)

▶ Labour plus other costs – The cost of this job is the labour cost (as just described) plus other costs – things like, travel, hotels, equipment, software, consumables, raw materials and so on. How can you estimate these? Three possibilities – ask a supplier, go look on the Internet, make an assumption.

▶ Subcontract – You are going to pay some supplier a fee to get this job done. In general, in this situation, you don't care how much work the supplier puts into it – since they are getting their fee. What you *do* care about though is how long the job is going to take, i.e. its duration and when it will actually be done.

Adding the budget for each individual job gives you the budget for the entire project. Easy as that.

WHO SAID IT

"**Blackadder:** You see, Baldrick, in order to prevent war in Europe, two superblocks developed: us, the French and Russians on one side, and the Germans and Austro-Hungary on the other. The idea was to have two vast opposing armies, each acting as the other's deterrent. That way, there could never be a war.

Baldrick: But this is sort of a war, isn't it, sir?

Blackadder: Yes, that's right. You see, there was only one tiny flaw in the plan.

George: What was that, sir?

Blackadder: It was b****cks."

ASSUMPTIONS

As mentioned previously, the big problem in project management is that you have to predict the future. Another way to think about this problem is that you never have enough *knowledge* about the project. Or to be more precise, the only day you have complete knowledge about the project is the day that it ends – and then this knowledge is of no use.

Assumptions are useful things – indeed, they are very powerful things – because you make up knowledge. You pretend to know things that you don't. Here's an example. Let's say that your project has some kind of testing phase in it. I'm not necessarily talking about technology projects here. Most projects have a part in them where you test that what you've done is good. Ask somebody to estimate this part of their project and they'll probably say something like, 'How long is a piece of string?' or 'It'll take as long as it takes.' Their rationale is that since they don't know how many errors they're going to find when they come to test it, it is impossible for them to say anything other than 'it'll take as long as it takes'.

But with assumptions you can do much better than this. You can assume that you'll find twenty, fifty or a thousand errors, or that ten percent of things tested will have errors in them or 9.714 percent. You can assume whatever you like. If these assumptions can be based on what happened on previous projects, so much the better. Otherwise you just make up something that sounds reasonable. It's no more complicated than that. But then see what this gets you:

1. First testing run (assume 10% errors)
2. Fix these errors
3. Second testing run (assume 5% errors)
4. Fix these errors
5. Third and final testing run (assume no errors).

WHO YOU NEED TO KNOW
Henry Laurence Gantt

Henry Laurence Gantt (1861–1919) was an American mechanical engineer and management consultant. He is most famous for developing the Gantt Chart, a way of representing plans and schedules. These charts were used, for example, on major US infrastructure projects such as the Hoover Dam and the Interstate highway system in the years before WWII. They are widely used today.

The assumptions enable you to add detail to your plan, which is a good thing.

There will come a time when you have to explain to the stakeholders what things are definite (i.e. knowledge) and what things are assumption. But this is not that time. For now you can treat knowledge and assumptions the same. So, if you come to estimate a piece of your project, and you say, 'I haven't a clue. I have no idea. We haven't decided this, we haven't decided that, so I have no way of knowing' – just make some assumptions and you will be able to estimate this piece of your project in great detail.

GANTT CHARTS

The Gantt Chart is one of the most common ways of representing a plan. It is a who-does-what-when representation of the plan. There are of course other representations. A budget, for example, is a who-spends-what-when representation of a plan and a cash flow forecast is a who-spends-what-when-and-who-earns-what-when representation of a plan.

There are a bunch of columns down the left hand side and then a calendar on the right. For the Gantt Charts

Example of a Gantt Chart

ID	❶	Task Name	Duration	Start	Finish	Predece
1		1 Finalize list of projects	3 days	Wed 05/11/03	Fri 07/11/03	
2		2 Establish Quality System Review Team	3 days	Wed 05/11/03	Fri 07/11/03	
3		**3 IMPROVEMENT**	**90 days**	**Mon 10/11/03**	**Fri 12/03/04**	
4		3.1 Gather problems with the process	60 days	Mon 10/11/03	Fri 30/01/04	1, 2
5		3.2 Improve the process as a result of 3.1	20 days	Mon 02/02/04	Fri 27/02/04	4
6		3.3 Report (to EVERYONE) regularly	90 days	Mon 10/11/03	Fri 12/03/04	1, 2
7		3.4 Release the new version (decide format)	10 days	Mon 01/03/04	Fri 12/03/04	5
8		3.5 Put out proposed changes to client	20 days	Mon 02/02/04	Fri 27/02/04	
9		**4 COMPLIANCE & IMPROVEMENT**	**100 days**	**Mon 05/01/04**	**Fri 21/05/04**	
10		4.1 Monitor implementation of the process	100 days	Mon 05/01/04	Fri 21/05/04	

that we're going to build we initially need columns for the following information. (More columns will be added later.)

► The description of the job itself.
► The work (in person-hours or person-days or some such measure) required to do that job.
► The duration of the job – how long it's going to take and when it will start and end.
► The other jobs that this job depends on. For example, this job might not be able to begin until some other job or jobs have finished.
► The budget – the cost of this job.

SOME USEFUL APPROXIMATIONS

When you're estimating you'll find the following to be of use to you. They're approximations but they make the arithmetic easy and they're close enough for government work (!), as the saying goes.

► Never mind that your contract says you have to work 37.5 or whatever it is, hours per week. For most estimating purposes 8 hours = 1 day or 8 person-hours (MH) = 1 person-day (MD).
► 5 days in a week, 5 person-days (PD) = 1 person-week (PW). (The prefix 'man-' and 'person-' used interchangeably with no offence intended to anybody,)

HOW YOU NEED TO DO IT
Good Estimating

Here's the method for doing good estimating:

1. Get the people who are going to do the project to do the estimating. If that can't be done because maybe they haven't all been hired or assigned or identified, then use the people who have. If you don't know who's going to do the project, get somebody to help you. Maybe a colleague can help you when you estimate and you can help them when they estimate. If there are people who have done such projects before, see if you can tap into their knowledge. If there are specialist parts of the project (IT, for example) involve the people who have the specialist knowledge. The worst thing you can do is to do all the estimating by yourself. The more heads you have working on the problem, the smaller the error there will be in the estimates.

2. Identify the big pieces of work that have to be done to get the project done. You don't have to be all that accurate here. You're just trying to break a bigger problem down into smaller

problems. You maybe don't know much about astrophysics, for example, but you can come up – pretty quickly – with the big pieces of work that have to be done to put a space probe on Venus. They're something like this:

- ▶ Put the space probe in a rocket.
- ▶ Shoot the rocket up in the air.
- ▶ Send it to Venus.
- ▶ Put it in an orbit around Venus.
- ▶ Take the space probe out.
- ▶ Put it down gently on the planet.
- ▶ Press 'Start'!

3. Notice that the big pieces of work give you natural 'milestones'. Milestones in project management are markers that you can put into your plan to give you a sense of what kind of progress you are making. The end of each of these big pieces of work could be treated a milestone.

4. Within each of these big pieces of work, identify the detailed jobs that have to be done.

5. Break everything down such that each job you identify is between 1-5 days duration or 1–5 person-days of work.

55

6. For each detailed job, be as specific and concrete as possible i.e. rather than saying 'requirements gathering' say 'Charlie meets with the IT people for two days to explain his requirements'. Using simple language to describe jobs is a good way to ensure this. Write the list of jobs so that a child could understand it.

7. Use cause and effect. This is just a fancy way of saying that jobs don't exist in isolation and that each job triggers other jobs. So there are really two questions to ask. The first one is 'what happens first?' Then, having written that job down, keep asking, 'what happens next?' or 'who does what?' until you've built your list (sequence) of jobs.

8. Where you don't know something, make an assumption.

9. List all the jobs in a structure which shows the project as being made up of the big pieces of work, which in turn are made up of the smaller pieces. This is what is known in project management jargon as a Work Breakdown Structure or WBS.

10. Lay all this information out in a Gantt Chart with the five columns as described previously.

▶ 20 days in a month, 20 person-days (PD) = 1 person-month (PM)

▶ 12 months in a year, 12 person-months (PM) = 1 person-year (PY)

▶ And finally, while it varies from country to country what with holiday entitlements and number of public holidays, but 240 person-days (MD) = 1 person-year (MY) is good enough for most situations.

CRITICAL PATH

You'll come across the term 'critical path' sooner or later. Lots of people use it; most do so incorrectly. Some people don't know what it means but use it anyway (at meetings, for example) because it sounds important – and thus, makes *them* sound important. Some use it to describe the critical things that have to be done on the project. This, however, is not the meaning of critical path.

The critical path is the shortest time in which a project can be done. Given that people are almost always under pressure to get projects done more quickly, knowing the critical path is essential if you are under such pressure.

Look at the following example. The critical path for job 6 is the 17 days that make up the sequence of jobs 6.1 through 6.6.

Plan with a critical path of 17 days

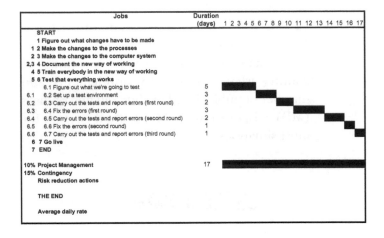

Jobs	Duration (days)	1 2 3 4 5 6 7 8 9 10 11 12 13 14 15 16 17
START		
1 Figure out what changes have to be made		
1 2 Make the changes to the processes		
2 3 Make the changes to the computer system		
2,3 4 Document the new way of working		
4 5 Train everybody in the new way of working		
5 6 Test that everything works		
6.1 Figure out what we're going to test	5	
6.1 6.2 Set up a test environment	3	
6.2 6.3 Carry out the tests and report errors (first round)	2	
6.3 6.4 Fix the errors (first round)	3	
6.4 6.5 Carry out the tests and report errors (second round)	2	
6.5 6.6 Fix the errors (second round)	1	
6.6 6.7 Carry out the tests and report errors (third round)	1	
6 7 Go live		
7 END		
10% Project Management	17	
15% Contingency		
Risk reduction actions		
THE END		
Average daily rate		

If you want to shorten a project, which you may well want to do, you need to shorten the critical path. How might that work in the example above? How could you shorten the 17 days? Well, one obvious way would be to say that you wouldn't wait for the testing to end before fixing begins. You might decide that after a day's testing (during the first round of testing), you would let the fixing people loose on whatever errors had been found that far. If you did that then here's what the plan could look like, shown on the following page.

It shortens the project by a day i.e. it shortens the critical path by one day.

Plan with the critical path shortened by a day

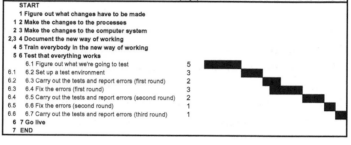

Jobs	Duration (days)	1 2 3 4 5 6 7 8 9 10 11 12 13 14 15 16
START		
1 Figure out what changes have to be made		
1 2 Make the changes to the processes		
2 3 Make the changes to the computer system		
2,3 4 Document the new way of working		
4 5 Train everybody in the new way of working		
5 6 Test that everything works		
6.1 Figure out what we're going to test	5	
6.1 6.2 Set up a test environment	3	
6.2 6.3 Carry out the tests and report errors (first round)	2	
6.3 6.4 Fix the errors (first round)	3	
6.4 6.5 Carry out the tests and report errors (second round)	2	
6.5 6.6 Fix the errors (second round)	1	
6.6 6.7 Carry out the tests and report errors (third round)	1	
6 7 Go live		
7 END		

Here's another example:

Another Critical Path example

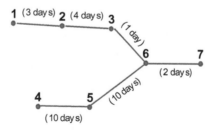

The critical path in this example is 22 days – the sequence 4–5–6–7. If you want to shorten this project, there's no point in messing about with jobs on the 1–2–3–6 path. If you shorten any of these it will have no effect on the length of the project. But if you were to shorten jobs 4–5, 5–6 or 6–7, then it would.

HOW MUCH PROJECT MANAGEMENT DOES THE PROJECT NEED?

There is one other thing that you need to consider at this point. Just because you can make a detailed list of jobs, estimate them and sequence them all together, it doesn't mean that they're just going to happen or get done. The jobs will only get done if somebody makes sure they get done. That is what the project manager is needed for.

This means then that, in every project you do, there needs to be a job called 'project management'. And, as you know now, if there is a job it needs to be estimated. So how do you estimate the job of project management?

Here's an easy rule of thumb to enable you to do that. Take the total work in the project (the work, *not* the duration) and calculate 10% of it. This should be enough to cover the project management.

Let's take a simple example. Let's say there are five people working on the project full-time and it lasts four months (duration). Then the total work in the project is 20 person-months (PM) – each of the five people puts in four months' work which gives a total of 20 PM. 10 per cent of that is 2 PM. So the total size of this project is 22 PM, 20 PM to do the project and 2 PM to make sure the project gets done.

And taking this just a little further, if this 2 PM takes place over the four months' duration of the project, then it's a half-time job ($2/4 = ½$) for somebody to run this project. And why this is important is because if somebody is spending half their time running this project, i.e. 2½ days per week, then they're only available half their time to do work on the project. This raises for the first time the issue of people's *availability*, i.e. time availability. This important issue will be covered several times in the course of the book.

Just to finish off then, a job called 'Project Management' must be added to the plan, shown on the following page. Its work will be the number calculated using the 10% rule, and its duration will be the duration of the project, starting on the first day and finishing on the last day. It has no dependencies i.e. no other jobs depend on it and it depends on no other jobs.

PROJECT MANAGEMENT METHODOLOGIES

In your project management travels it won't be long before you come across the 'm' word – methodologies. Traditional, Critical Chain (CCPM), Extreme/Agile, Proprietary methodologies, PRINCE2 and lots of others. What are these things and what is their significance to you?

Plan with 'Project Management' job added

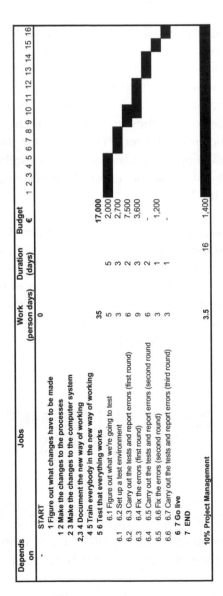

Depends on	Jobs	Work (person days)	Duration (days)	Budget €	1 2 3 4 5 6 7 8 9 10 11 12 13 14 15 16
-	START	0			
	1 Figure out what changes have to be made				
1	2 Make the changes to the processes				
2	3 Make the changes to the computer system				
2,3	4 Document the new way of working				
4	5 Train everybody in the new way of working				
5	6 Test that everything works	35		17,000	
	6.1 Figure out what we're going to test	5	5	2,000	
6.1	6.2 Set up a test environment	3	3	2,700	
6.2	6.3 Carry out the tests and report errors (first round)	6	2	7,500	
6.3	6.4 Fix the errors (first round)	9	3	3,600	
6.4	6.5 Carry out the tests and report errors (second round)	6	2	-	
6.5	6.6 Fix the errors (second round)	3	1	1,200	
6.6	6.7 Carry out the tests and report errors (third round)	3	1	-	
6	7 Go live				
7	END				
	10% Project Management	3.5	16	1,400	

Project management methodologies are essentially big processes. They are attempts to state all of the steps somebody has to go through to carry out a project. Some methodologies are proprietary – unique to a particular company or organisation – and some are more widely available. In Britain, for example, the PRINCE2 methodology is particularly popular and widely used, especially in government bodies and large organisations.

It's perhaps worth saying too that a lot of these methodologies have their origins in the areas of software development and IT. Given that these areas are not renowned for their project success rates, it might beg the question what value these methodologies add.

Anyway, the big question for you is that if there are all these methodologies out there why would you need a book like this? Why not pick some methodology and just use it? Here's why.

This book doesn't describe yet another methodology. It does not compete with existing methodologies. Rather it describes best *practice* in project management. Things like establishing the goal of the project, as covered in Chapter 1, estimating as covered in this chapter, and the things that will be discussed in later chapters (particularly Chapter 5) are essential if your project is to succeed.

But don't the methodologies all get you to carry out this best practice, you may well ask? Well no, the fact is that they don't. There is obviously a lot of overlap between what is covered here and the methodologies. But there is no methodology that will give you what you are getting here – an approach that:

▶ Works. (Nobody has ever phoned me up and said, 'I did it and it didn't work.').
▶ Is common sense – simple to learn and easy to use.
▶ Is 'light' – tells you the absolute *least* you have to do to have a successful project.

I have also seen no correlation between the use of a particular methodology and successful projects.

There are a bewildering number of methodologies out there. For example, here's a list of methodologies from googling 'project management methodologies comparison'. (And this is without going near proprietary ones – ones that are unique to particular organisations.)

▶ Adaptive Project Framework
▶ Agile Software Development
▶ Critical Chain (CCPM)
▶ Crystal Methods
▶ Dynamic Systems Development Model
▶ Extreme Programming

▶ Feature Driven Development
▶ Information Technology Infrastructure Library (ITIL)
▶ Joint Application Development
▶ Lean Development
▶ PRINCE2
▶ Rapid Application Development
▶ Rational Unified Process
▶ Scrum
▶ Spiral
▶ Systems Development Life Cycle
▶ Waterfall (Traditional).

Now you can see just from the sound of these that a lot of them are to do with developing software or IT systems. So are they even project management methodologies at all or are they rather methodologies for developing [computer] systems?

So what should you do? Well, first of all this is not to rubbish methodologies. There are lots of good things in them – checklists, forms, templates, procedures that can make your life easier and stop you from having to reinvent the wheel. So if you find yourself in a situation where one is available, be sure to check it out to see what in it might be useful to you. Also you may find yourself in a situation where following a certain methodology is mandatory. In either case, just make sure that you don't stray from the essential principles of good project management that are being laid down in these chapters.

PROJECT MANAGEMENT TOOLS

The other thing that you'll run into as soon as you start to run projects is the whole business of project management tools and the ubiquitous Microsoft Project. What's the story with these?

Well, if you think about it, to do pretty much anything in life, you need a method and you need some tools. To cook dinner, for instance, you need a method – a recipe – and then you need tools – a cooker, pots and pans, a knife and so on. It's the same with project management. This book is giving you the *method*. You should then choose whatever tool(s) you need to help you to best get the job done. Furthermore, you should use the simplest tool(s) that will get the job done. So:

You can use pieces of paper, white or black boards, flip chart pages or butcher paper. It's perhaps worth remembering that the tool the Egyptians had available to them was papyrus rolls and look what they did. World War One was won and lost without a computer. Enormous projects can and have been planned and executed using plans written on bits of paper.

The big drawback of paper, of course, is updating. As your project begins, as things begin to change, as your plan needs to be updated, a plan written on paper can become very messy and time-consuming to update. So then you could use something like Word (or whatever equivalent you use.)

Better again is Excel (or whatever equivalent you use). It was never intended for it, but it's great for drawing and updating plans. Its only drawback really is that it's not good at showing dependencies between jobs. (Which is fair enough, since it's a spreadsheet, not a project planning tool.)

Getting more fancy again, you can move on into project planning tools. Microsoft Project is the most commonly used. There are others and you can get free ones on the Internet. They do some things very well – MS Project is terrific, for example, at helping to build lists of jobs (Work Breakdown Structures) very quickly.

Finally, there are very expensive, enterprise-wide project planning tools such as Primavera or MS Project Server and lots more.

You'll find that each of these tools, ranging from the simplest right up to the very fancy, has advantages and disadvantages. It's worth mentioning that you can also use combinations of tools, harnessing the strengths of each and reducing the effect of their weaknesses. Thus, you could build a plan showing durations in MS Project but calculate the work and budget in Excel. It may involve having to enter information twice but the resulting flexibility you get is worth the effort.

It's also worth saying that for small projects, a plan on a bit of paper could be perfectly adequate, whereas for some vast undertaking, it's almost certainly better to use a computer.

WHAT YOU NEED TO READ

▶ The Prince2 website (*www.prince2.com*) will tell you all you need to know about the PRINCE2 methodology. In many organisations, both in the UK and in a number of Commonwealth countries (e.g. Australia), PRINCE2 is used and having a qualification in PRINCE2 can be a requirement to be a project manager in that organisation. If you work in software, IT or have to deal with these people, then it probably won't be long before you start to hear them talk about 'agile', 'agile methodologies', 'extreme programming' and other delights. Get ahead of them, find out what they're on about and be able to nail them with tricky questions by checking out these sites – *www.agilemanifesto.org* or *www.agilealliance.org*.

▶ The Comparison of Project Management Software entry on Wikipedia (*http://en.wikipedia.org/wiki/comparison_of_project_management_software*) is a good place to start if you want to go exploring the world of project management tools and software. If you want to try out some free software then just google on things like 'free project management software' or 'free project planning software'. If you want to try out Microsoft Project – purely on the basis that it's popular and widely used – you can get a free 60-day trial at the Microsoft Project website (*www.microsoft.com/project*). Many other suppliers offer trials as well.

▶ Yes, *How to Run Successful Projects III* (Addison Wesley, 2001) is one of my other books on project management. I'm only going to mention two in this book and this is one of them. First published in 1994, it's now in its third edition so there must be some useful stuff in it.

▶ There are three books about the film-making industry which are interesting to project managers because film-making is an industry that estimates huge projects very well. Yes, there are famous movie overrun stories such as the making of 'Ryan's Daughter' or 'Heaven's Gate', but these days movie projects are run with a precision that would keep any accountant happy. The three books are:

▶ *My Indecision is Final: The Rise and Fall of Goldcrest Films* by Jake Eberts (Faber & Faber, 1992);

▶ *Money into Light: The Emerald Forest Diary* by John Boorman (Faber & Faber, 1986);

▶ And *Final Cut: Dreams and Disaster in the making of 'Heaven's Gate'* by Stephen Bach (Faber & Faber, 1986)

IF YOU ONLY REMEMBER ONE THING

The devil *is* in the detail. If you don't figure out the detail in your project at the beginning, it will come back to haunt you later on.

CHAPTER 3

SUPPLY AND DEMAND

WHAT IT'S ALL ABOUT

- ▶ Project management is a problem in supply and demand
- ▶ Why every job must have somebody to do it
- ▶ Availability – the silent killer of projects
- ▶ How to calculate availability
- ▶ What dance cards are
- ▶ How to play to the strengths (and to the weaknesses!) of the team

PROJECT MANAGEMENT IS A PROBLEM IN SUPPLY AND DEMAND

Like many things in life, project management is a problem in supply and demand. We're all familiar with supply and demand problems. There is our income [supply] and the cost of our lifestyle [demand]. If supply is greater than or equal to demand, we're in business. If supply is less than demand, we're in trouble. It's the same with project management.

In theory it's all really simple. If there are 100 person-days (PD) worth of work to be done [demand] there's got to be 100 PD worth of people to do the work [supply].

Just before going on, a little note here for accuracy. To be really precise here the chapter should talk about 'resources' rather than people. Some jobs require just people to get them done, i.e. they require only animate resources. But sometimes jobs require other resources as well – equipment, travel, consumables, machinery, things like that – inanimate resources. This chapter will focus on animate resources because that's where 99% of the problems occur. It's unusual to come across a project that gets into trouble because it couldn't get enough inanimate resources – two desks, four computers and a particular piece of software, for example. Projects get into trouble because they couldn't get enough animate resources to do all the work. Now, it's probably better to call animate resources people and so that's where the focus will be in this chapter. But just bear in mind that sometimes you need other resources as well.

Okay, in theory, it's very simple. 100 PD demand. 100 PD supply.

The difficulty arises, though, from the combination of two effects. First, the demand has a tendency to go up. Stakeholders ask for more things, extra things, 'Can it do this?', 'Can I have that?', 'I thought we were getting that as well.' It's also worth pointing out that if the goal of your project was unclear in the first place, this will almost invariably cause demand to go up.

And then if that wasn't bad enough, the supply has a tendency to go do down. There are never quite enough people. Or they arrive on the project later than they were meant to. Or you get them, but then they get pulled back into some other project. Or they're on your project, but they're also involved in some other project and you don't get all of their time that you expected.

So supply and demand tend to go out of balance. Demand goes up, supply goes down. If the two things go out of balance and they stay out of balance, then your project will crash and burn. You may have heard the expression, 'it's not black and white', and many things in life aren't black and white. Unfortunately supply and demand *is* black and white. If there aren't enough people to do all the work, you may as well go home.

It's worth saying too that you sometimes hear people use the expression 'estimate resource requirements'. In a sense, this is a stupid thing to say. With resources there's no estimation. The estimation comes when you estimate how much work has to be done – the demand. Once you've done that, there's no estimation – it's just an equation. Whatever the demand is that you've estimated there has to be an equal amount of supply. End of story.

Just as with the goal in chapter 1, there are three issues that are important. These three issues also belong on the list of major project killers. Here they are in turn:

1. EVERY JOB MUST HAVE SOMEBODY TO DO IT

Now you're probably looking at this section heading and saying, 'For heaven's sake, we know this. You don't have to tell us this.' Well unfortunately, I *do* have to tell you this because it seems there are lots of people out there who believe that this doesn't apply to them. Allow me to illustrate.

A few years ago I was making a sales call on an IT Manager to sell him project management training. While I was in his office this project manager came in and said to the IT manager, his boss, 'I just wanted to remind you that it's exactly three months from today to the day when testing on my project is due to start. If you remember, my plan said that I needed two test engineers. So I just wanted to give you plenty of notice so that you could get Human Resources started on finding the two test engineers.' Good stuff from the project manager – giving the boss plenty of notice.

The boss then says, 'You know we have a hiring freeze on at the moment so that I can't hire anybody.' Good stuff from the boss – this is the kind of things bosses say all the time.

The project manager then puts a sort of puzzled look on his face, thinks for a few moments, then says, 'Okay' and walks out. This is a big black mark to the project manager.

There are a few things to be learnt from this story but perhaps the most important one is to ask the question, 'What did the boss hear?' The answer is that the boss heard that there wouldn't be a problem. Somehow this job of testing [demand] which had nobody to do it [supply] would get done.

Think back to Chapter 1 and the three possible responses to changes on projects:

▶ Big change.
▶ Use contingency.
▶ Suck it up.

From this, it's clear how this change is going to be dealt with. There'll be plenty of sucking it up on this project. The project manager's development engineers by day will be test engineers by night and at weekends.

And just in conclusion, notice that the project manager's correct response should have been to declare this a big change – as it clearly is. His response should have been, 'Okay, no problem boss. I'll be back to you shortly with the plan for the project based on no test engineers and you can tell me what you think of that.'

So – you've got to have people to do the work. There has to be supply to match demand.

It's completely likely that say, at the beginning of the project, you may not know who's going to work on what. And so you may have to put into your plan, in the column labelled 'Who' (as shown on the next page), descriptions of the kind of skill or person you need.

So you may write things like 'New hire' or 'TBD [To be decided] or TBH [To be hired] or 'Engineer number 2' or 'Financial specialist' or 'Java programmer' or 'Contractor' – so-called 'generic resources'. But at the risk of stating the obvious, before a particular job is due to start, a generic resource had to be replaced by a warm, living, loving human being – or else the job won't get done.

Example of a Gantt Chart with 'Who' column added

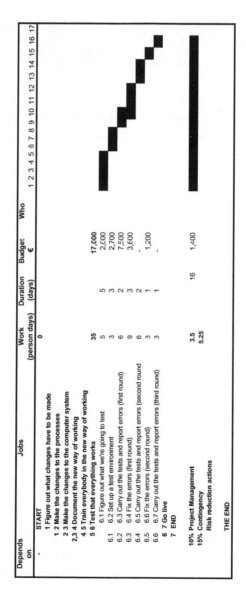

Depends on	Jobs	Work (person days)	Duration (days)	Budget €	Who	1 2 3 4 5 6 7 8 9 10 11 12 13 14 15 16 17
-	START	0				
	1 Figure out what changes have to be made					
1	2 Make the changes to the processes					
2	3 Make the changes to the computer system					
2,3	4 Document the new way of working					
	5 Train everybody in the new way of working					
	6 Test that everything works	35		17,000		
	6.1 Figure out what we're going to test	5	5	2,000		
6.1	6.2 Set up a test environment	3	3	2,700		
6.2	6.3 Carry out the tests and report errors (first round)	6	2	7,500		
6.3	6.4 Fix the errors (first round)	9	3	3,600		
6.4	6.5 Carry out the tests and report errors (second round)	6	2	-		
6.5	6.6 Fix the errors (second round)	3	1	1,200		
6.6	6.7 Carry out the tests and report errors (third round)	3	1	-		
	6 7 Go live					
	7 END					
	10% Project Management	3.5				
	15% Contingency	5.25	16	1,400		
	Risk reduction actions					
	THE END					

2. AVAILABILITY – THE SILENT KILLER OF PROJECTS

Then – the second of the three issues – it isn't enough that you have people; those people have to have enough time to devote to the project. So here's a terrifying calculation.

Let's say that there's a job that has to be done on your project and you estimate it to be 10 person-days. Charlie's going to do it and Charlie's available full time i.e. 5 days a week. Then the duration of this job is 2 weeks – 5 days the first week, 5 days the second week, job done.

Now supposing it was to happen that Charlie was only available one day a week and you know how easily this can occur. Charlie is involved in another project which was meant to have finished but it hasn't quite finished yet, so he has to spend time there. And Charlie is the only guy who knows about the X project or system or thing and there are some issues with that. And there's been a customer-related issue that Charlie's having to deal with … You know how it goes.

With 1 day a week, Charlie's job will take 10 weeks. And this doesn't take into account that the job will now probably be bigger than 10 MD now, because there is going to be the additional effect of Charlie putting it down and picking it up a week later. But never mind about that for now. This thing of we-estimated-5-days-a-week-we-got-1, doesn't sound that serious. On a big project you mightn't even pick up that it had happened. Hell, on a small project, with Charlie sitting behind you, you mightn't pick up that it had happened. Yet, this one little thing, that doesn't appear that serious, can potentially cause a *two month* delay on this project (10 weeks minus 2 weeks).

Some of the things discussed so far – not knowing the goal of the project, not doing proper change control, bad estimating and so on – these are big elephant-in-the-room type things. It can be hard to miss them. But you can miss this. Not knowing people's correct availability will just eat away at your project. You'll start and almost immediately, you'll start to fall behind schedule. The team will start to work a bit harder, longer hours, more sucking it up. But it won't do any good. You'll continue to slip. You'll be sending out status reports saying things like, 'We've lost a bit of ground but we hope to make it up later in the project' – one of life's greatest illusions. One day you wake up and you're miles adrift of where you expected to be. Scary, huh?

So you need to know people's real availability. How to do that is described in the next section.

Calculating Availability

Most people don't know their availability. Worse than that people have a tendency to *overestimate* their availability. How this then tends to manifest itself is as follows.

Your boss comes along to you and asks, 'Can you give me some time to do this particular thing next week?' Most people just automatically say 'yes' or 'sure'. If you're a bit more canny – which hopefully you're starting to become at this stage - you ask, 'Exactly how much time do you need?' 'A day,' he says. At that point, more than likely, you say, 'Sure.'

Now it may be that in saying 'sure', you have done both you and your boss a great disservice. To him you may have promised something – the one day – that you don't actually have. For yourself, you may have taken an already heavy overload and increased it even further. And all of this because you didn't know your availability.

So you have to know your real availability and here's how to calculate that. You need to do a Dance Card. A what? Read on.

DANCE CARDS

The Dance Card (also known as a Supply-Demand Calculator) is a reference to those more genteel times where, when women went to dances or balls, they were given a card with a list of the tunes that the band or orchestra was going to play. To dance with a woman a gentleman wrote his name against a particular dance, i.e. he booked that dance with that woman. The Dance Card measured supply (the number of dances available) and demand (the number of dances booked).

To calculate your Dance Card, you need to figure out your supply and your demand. Here's how to do that:

Figuring Out Demand

In order to figure out your demand, you need to pick a period of time and then make a list of all the projects that you will be working on during that period. These projects should include anything within that timeframe regardless of when it actually starts and ends. For example, you would include a project that starts during the period, one that starts and ends in that period, or runs through the period that you have chosen.

Your current workload and day-to-day tasks also need to be accounted for when figuring out demand, so the next stage will be to add your 'business-as-usual' tasks to your list. These would be things like:

> ▶ Meetings – All your meetings may be about particular projects, but most of us have things like 'the group meeting', the Monday meeting', 'company meeting' and so on. Don't forget too

that you may have to do preparation before a meeting, there will be the meeting itself and you may have to do follow-ups or action items afterwards.

▶ Reports – Maybe your job involves producing (or reading) a lot of these.

▶ Interruptions – Whether they come person-to-person or by phone (landline or mobile), every one of us has these every day.

▶ Inbox/E-mail – Possibly all of your e-mails are related to specific projects, but most of us have other stuff we have to deal with every day. And anyway, there's the time involved in figuring out whether they're about specific projects or not.

▶ Trips/Visits – Maybe you're going on a business-related trip or somebody's coming to visit you and that will soak up your time.

▶ Training – Maybe you're involved in some form of training course or you're coaching or men-toring somebody else.

▶ Annual leave/vacation/holidays

▶ Day job – Maybe you already have a full time job and you have been landed with a project load on top of that.

▶ Managing people – Maybe you're the line manager of some bunch of people and this takes up your time.

▶ Phone calls/conference calls – We all have some / a lot of these to do every day.

▶ Support – Maybe you support products or systems or people in some way.

- ▶ Recruitment – Maybe your organisation is expanding and you have to spend time looking at resumes, interviewing people and doing related activities.
- ▶ Fire fighting
- ▶ Filling in for people – Maybe you're standing in for people who are away on some kind of leave.

Finally, you also need to factor in the inevitable fact that new things are likely to come up during the period. How often has your boss come in to you and said something to the effect of, 'never mind all that – this new thing is far more important'? It may be that in your job nothing is going to change over the period that you're looking at. (I've heard there are jobs like that though I've never come across one myself!) However, what's more likely is that new things will come along. You don't know what they are yet because they haven't come along – you just know it's inevitable that they will. So you'll need to add an additional line called 'New stuff' to cover these.

You'll then need to figure out how much of your time is going to go into each of the items on your list over the period that you're looking at. Use hours per day, days per week, total, hours, total days or whatever measure seems most appropriate to each line item. Be sure to record each of the amounts of time in the same units. Days are probably best for this.

Add all of these up. This gives you the total amount of work you have to do in the period in question.

HOW YOU NEED TO DO IT
How to Figure Out Demand

1. Pick a period of time.
2. Make a list of all the projects you will be working on during this period.
3. Add to the list what might be called 'business as usual' or 'day-job' type things.
4. Add an additional line item called, 'New stuff'.
5. Work out how much time (in hours or days) will be taken up by each of the items and add this up to figure out the total amount of work.

Figuring Out Supply

Supply is the amount of time you have available. In order for you to do all the work you have to do (demand) properly, there has to be an equal amount of supply. So you need to work this out as well. It'll be based on the number of days a week and the number of hours per day that you work. Thus, if you work say, a 5-day week but only work mornings from 8:30–12:30 (4 hours), then your supply will be $5 \times 4 = 20$ hours or 2.5 days. This is how much time you have available.

HOW YOU NEED TO DO IT
How to Figure Out Supply

1. Use the same period of time for which you calculated demand.
2. Figure out how many of your work days there are in that period. (Remember to exclude any public holidays.)
3. Multiply this by the number of hours a day that you work.
4. This is your supply in hours. If your demand was calculated in hours then you're done. Otherwise, if your demand was calculated in days, convert this to days by dividing by 8.

3. PLAYING TO THE STRENGTHS (AND NOT PLAYING TO THE WEAKNESSES!) OF THE TEAM

Finally, it's not enough that you have people, it's not enough that they have availability. The final thing is that they better bloody know what they're doing. Or to put it in a more tactful, human resources kind of way, you should play to their strengths and not to their weaknesses.

Maybe when you were a kid you were really good at games (a superstar) and you were always one of the first people to be picked on any team. Or maybe you were just okay (a good citizen) and so it took a while before the people doing the picking got to you. Or maybe you were awful at games (a loose cannon) and it essentially didn't matter to the people doing the picking whose team you ended up on.

It's exactly the same when people are assigned to your team. You may have a superstar type situation – the person is skilled, motivated and there's very little doubt that they won't get the job done. You may have good citizens – not as reliable as the superstars, but by and large, they do a good job. And you may have the equivalent of loose cannons – people whose abilities or skills or motivation are in doubt. At the risk of stating the obvious, you want to try and match people as much as possible to the things they're good at and like to do. You're also going to have to manage these different types of people and situations differently. So let's look at a very simple way of doing this.

Harnessing the Strengths Of the Team

When you assign a job to a person, here's a very simple way you could rate the assignments. Notice two things. Firstly, this is going to highlight weaknesses in (and therefore threats to) your project. Second, you will be able to use this information when you come to run the project because it will guide you as to how to manage in different situations. More about that in Chapter 6.

It's important to say too that if you're going to do this rating, it needs to be based on *evidence* – so it's not about whether you like people or not. How could you gather this evidence? Well, pretty simply, really. Assuming you've broken jobs down to the level of detail talked about in Chapter 2, then after two or three weeks on the project it should be possible to build what you can think of as a 'report card' for each person, showing their performance on their jobs.

1. **Superstar.** This person is highly skilled and highly motivated to do this task. It's unlikely that there'll be any trouble getting this task done. The evidence appears to be that every time you give them a job it gets done. You can think of them as having a 'report card' that looks like this ✓✓✓✓✓✓✓.

2. **Good Citizen.** Their report card looks like this ✓✓✓X✓✓. Mostly they get things done.

3. **Don't Report To Me.** This can include people in other groups or departments, people who may be more senior than you, people you definitely have no control or authority over, people in other companies and organisations and subcontractors. The problem you're going to run into here is going to be one of priority i.e. what's important to you (jobs on your project) is not important to them – or at least, not sufficiently important. Mostly the issue will be that doing the job you want them to do will never rise high enough on their priority list. It may seem like you're doomed in this situation but never fear – as we'll see in Chapter 6, there is plenty you can do to deal with this situation.

4. **New To The Job.** As the name suggests, without watching, handholding, nurturing, training, on-the-job training, shadowing this person is more than likely going to turn in a report card of XXXXXX.

5. **No Availability.** A Dance Card check has shown that this person has no time available to do this particular job.

6. **Can't Do The Job.** The evidence is – report card shows – XXXXXX or something close to that.

You can see then, if you do this analysis, where some of the weaknesses in your project are going to lie.

WHO SAID IT

"You can't turn a herd of turtles into a twenty-mule work team."
– L. Todryk

WHO SAID IT

"It must be considered that there is nothing more difficult to carry out nor more doubtful of success nor more dangerous to handle than to initiate a new order of things."
– Niccolò Machiavelli

WHO YOU NEED TO KNOW
Pierre Paul Riquet

Pierre Paul Riquet is the man responsible for building the Canal du Midi, the oldest functioning canal in Europe. The Canal du Midi was/is the canal that linked / links the ocean (the Atlantic) to the sea (the Mediterranean).

Over the centuries, starting with the Romans, people had discussed the possibility of doing this but the difficulties of water management at points many hundreds of metres above sea level and far away from rivers made it seem impossible.

Riquet had a combination of skills that would be the envy of any project manager. He had the vision of the goal (as described in Chapter 1), the imagination to solve previously intractable engineering problems, the dedication and enthusiasm to drive the project through to completion. Riquet was a model leader, taking care of the health and well-being of his 12,000 or so project team members. (It's also worth mentioning that he funded the project himself.)

On top of all this, the project delivered something of great beauty – *harmonieux* is the word the French would use. If you ever get a chance, walk beside or sail along it. You'll be entranced by the beauty of the bridges, locks, tunnels, cuttings and the trees planted beside it. Go to the city of Beziers and marvel at the seven locks of Fonseranes which allow the canal to descend *21 metres* or the bridge that carries it over the River Orb.

WHAT YOU'VE ACHIEVED

It's time to take a break and assess what you've achieved. Back in Chapter 1 it was said that whenever you get handed any kind of project, it usually comes packaged with some constraints – wishes that people have about how and when the project will be done. It was said that you had no way of knowing if these wishes were achievable until you had done some analysis of the project – just as any other professional would do when handed a problem in their field. You have now completed that analysis. So what do you have?

HOW YOU NEED TO DO IT
Adding People to Your Project

1. Add two extra columns to your Gantt Chart. The first one will be called 'Who', the second one will be called 'Availability'.
2. In the 'Who' column put in either generic resources (as described above) or people's names. Don't forget that for the generic resources you're going to have to get these people, so you should put into your plan the extra jobs required to hire or assign the people
3. Figure out people's availability. Use a Dance Card if you're not sure. Notice that people's availability may cause durations to change. For example
   you may have thought that a 5 person-day job could be done in a week because perhaps you thought somebody was working on it full time. If, when you check their availability and they're only available half-time (2½ days per week) the job is going to take twice as long – 2 weeks.

You have a plan – also known as a 'Project Plan'. If you'd ever wondered what a plan was before then now you know. A plan is three things:

1. What (exactly) are you trying to do?
2. What work has to be done to get you there
3. Who's going to do that stuff?

You can also think of this plan as a supply-demand model of the project. When we say 'model', think a working model, like a model railway or a piece of Lego Technic. It's a supply-demand model in the sense that you can vary the supply or demand and see the effect. You can say, for example, (on the demand side): what if the stakeholders don't want a glass but rather a swimming pool (remember the example in Chapter 1) – what will that do to the model? Equally, you can vary the supply – by saying, for example: what happens to the plan if I don't get my two test engineers, as discussed earlier?

So in a very real sense you have a *simulation* or a simulator of the project. Sometimes these plans are called 'project manager's flight simulators' and while that's a bit Californian, the idea that the plan is a simulation of the project is a useful idea. You may remember the estimating example from Chapter 2 – here it is again.

Any one of us could run section '6 Test that everything works' of this project now because we have simulated it. It's almost like we have lived through it and understand all the issues involved.

Estimating example from Chapter 2

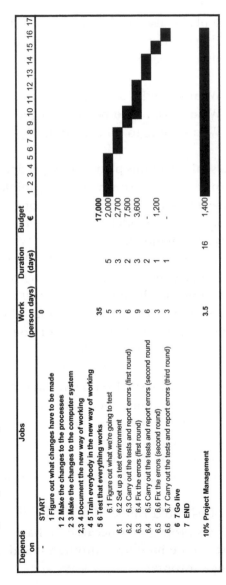

Depends on	Jobs	Work (person days)	Duration (days)	Budget €	1 2 3 4 5 6 7 8 9 10 11 12 13 14 15 16 17
-	START	0			
	1 Figure out what changes have to be made				
	1 2 Make the changes to the processes				
	2 3 Make the changes to the computer system				
	2,3 4 Document the new way of working				
	4 5 Train everybody in the new way of working	35		17,000	
	5 6 Test that everything works	5	5	2,000	
6.1	6.1 Figure out what we're going to test	3	3	2,700	
6.2	6.2 Set up a test environment	6	2	7,500	
6.3	6.3 Carry out the tests and report errors (first round)	9	3	3,600	
6.4	6.4 Fix the errors (first round)	6	2	-	
6.5	6.5 Carry out the tests and report errors (second round)	3	1	1,200	
6.6	6.6 Fix the errors (second round)	3	1	-	
	6.7 Carry out the tests and report errors (third round)				
	6 7 Go live				
	7 END				
	10% Project Management	3.5	16	1,400	

This plan, this model, this simulator can be represented in many different ways. The representation chosen here is a Gantt Chart – a who-does-what-when representation. But there are lots of other possible representations. A budget, for example, is a who-spends-what-when representation of the plan. A so-called network diagram represents the plan by showing the dependencies between the jobs and so it shows the sequence of work in the project and how the project is going to unfold. (Notice that looking at the right hand side of a Gantt Chart has the same effect.)

The other thing about your plan is that it connects four things which are really important and these are:

> **What** the project is delivering (the goal of the project – what's in the box).
> **When** the project will be done.
> **Work** – the amount of work (person-days) in the project (which in turn can lead you to the budget).
> **Quality** – there are a whole bunch of jobs in the project which are about ensuring that what you do isn't just on time and within budget, but is actually good. All of the jobs in '6 Test that everything works' are about this very thing.

So now you know everything you need to know.

You would have thought then that, at this point, you're ready to go and deal with the constraints. But there's one other thing you have to do before you do that. You have to realise that this plan as it stands is an incredibly fragile thing. Think of it as a one-hour old baby. If you were to go with this plan, then as soon as the first little slip-up happens on the project – Charlie goes sick for a day, for example – you start to fall behind schedule and go over budget.

So what you have to do is to take this incredibly fragile plan and toughen it up. You have to get it ready to go out into the world. If it's like a one-hour old baby when you start, it's going to be like a nineteen year old with attitude when you finish. To do this you're going to put contingency in the plan and do risk management. They're in the next chapter.

WHAT YOU NEED TO READ

▶ If you want to find out more about teams, team building, what makes for good teams and all that kind of stuff, the Belbin website (*www.belbin.com/*) is a good place to start.

▶ ETP (*www.etpint.com*) has an Excel spreadsheet called a Supply-Demand Calculator that will enable you to do a Dance Card quickly.

▶ *Peopleware: Productive Projects and Teams* by Tom DeMarco & Timothy Lister (Dorset House, 1999) is mainly about people and teams in the software industry, but any project manager could benefit from this book.

▶ *Tony Soprano on Management* by Anthony Schneider (Berkeley Books, 2004) has an almost endless stream of good, sensible suggestions for getting things done.

IF YOU ONLY REMEMBER ONE THING

Jobs don't get done if there aren't people to do them!

CHAPTER 4
MANAGING RISK

WHAT IT'S ALL ABOUT

- ► What contingency is and how to use it
- ► What risk analysis is
- ► The way to assess a project in five minutes
- ► How to use the Probability of Success Indicator (PSI)

CONTINGENCY AND RISK ANALYSIS

As mentioned in the previous section you're going to have to toughen up your plan to get it ready to go out into the world. You're going to do that using two related, but different techniques – a belt and braces approach.

The first one, contingency, is a blunt instrument. Its view of the world is that of the Project Manager's Prayer mentioned in Chapter 1. Here it is again:

'Unexpected stuff happens on projects.
Most of it is bad unexpected stuff.
Sometimes I get a lucky break,
But mostly, it is bad unexpected stuff.
For this I need to have contingency in the plan.'

Risk Analysis then does a smarter thing. It says that in reality, some parts of the project are more risky than other parts. Wouldn't it be nice if you could figure out those parts and wouldn't it be even nicer if you could do something about them – if you could reduce or eliminate these risks?

And you're hoping then that the combination of things that you've done:

► Knowing precisely what you're trying to do (Chapter 1);

▶ Putting lots of detail and knowledge from previous projects (if you have it) in the plan (Chapter 2);

▶ Matching supply to demand (Chapter 3);

▶ Contingency to cover bad things that will inevitably happen (this chapter);

▶ Risk analysis to try to stop some of those bad things from happening (also this chapter);

will be enough to get the project done safely. And if you heard 'hoping', hoping was what was said – that's about as scientific as this gets.

WHO YOU NEED TO KNOW
Henri Fayol

Henri Fayol (1841–1825) was a French mining engineer and management theorist who put forward a general theory of management. He proposed that there were six primary functions of management. These were:

1. Forecasting
2. Planning
3. Organising

4. Commanding
5. Coordinating
6. Controlling

You can see that the first three are central to what has been covered so far. You'll find the other three in the chapters to come.

Fayol also identified what he called 14 principles of management. Almost all of them have relevance to project managers.

1. **Division of work**. This principle is the same as Adam Smith's 'division of labour'. Specialisation increases output by making employees more efficient.
2. **Authority**. Managers must be able to give orders. Authority gives them this right. Responsibility arises wherever authority is exercised.
3. **Discipline**. Employees must obey and respect the rules that govern the organisation. Good discipline is the result of effective leadership, a clear understanding between management and workers regarding the organisation's rules, and the judicious use of penalties for infractions of the rules.

4. **Unity of command**. Every employee should receive orders from only one superior.

5. **Unity of direction**. Each group of organisational activities that have the same objective should be directed by one manager using one plan. [Thus every project should have only one leader.]

6. **Subordination of individual interests to the general interest**. The interests of any one employee or group of employees should not take precedence over the interests of the organisation as a whole.

7. **Remuneration**. Workers must be paid a fair wage for their services.

8. **Centralisation**. Centralisation refers to the degree to which subordinates are involved in decision making. Whether decision making is centralised (to management) or decentralised (to subordinates) is a question of proper proportion. The task is to find the optimum degree of centralisation for each situation.

9. **Scalar chain**. The line of authority from top management to the lowest ranks represents the scalar chain. Communications should follow

this chain. However, if following the chain creates delays, cross-communications can be allowed if agreed to by all parties and superiors are kept informed.

10. **Order**. People and materials should be in the right place at the right time.

11. **Equity**. Managers should be kind and fair to their subordinates.

12. **Stability of tenure of personnel**. High employee turnover is inefficient. Management should provide orderly personnel planning and ensure that replacements are available to fill vacancies. [Hence, sucking it up/working burnout hours is a bad idea because it leads to high employee turnover.]

13. **Initiative**. Employees who are allowed to originate and carry out plans will exert high levels of effort. [Involve the people who will do the work in the estimating.]

14. **Esprit de corps**. Promoting team spirit will build harmony and unity within the organisation

CONTINGENCY – WHY YOU NEED IT

Let's get the most important point out of the way first. *You've got to have contingency in your plan.* If you don't have contingency in your plan then you lose one of your three possible responses to changes. You'll remember they were:

▶ Big change
▶ Use contingency
▶ Suck it up.

With contingency gone, you're left with:

▶ Big change
▶ Suck it up.

What this means is that every change that occurs on your project, which cannot be classed as a big change, is going to have to be dealt with by working longer hours, nights, weekends, all that kind of stuff. A terrible idea.

There's a simpler way to view it as well. If you don't have contingency in your plan then, logically, what conclusion can be drawn from that? Logically, the only conclusion that can be drawn from that is that you believe your plan is going to work out exactly like you said. Logically the only conclusion that can be drawn from that is that you're nuts! There has never been a plan in the history of the world that worked out exactly as its author said it would – and don't ever forget it!

CONTINGENCY – HIDDEN vs. EXPLICIT/ HOW MUCH AND HOW

The next decision you're going to have to make is whether you'll put the contingency in explicitly or hide it. There is an argument that says you put it in explicitly *and* you hide it. The powers-that-be get to take it out, you still have it in there and if you stop them from taking it out, you'll have twice as much! A good thing. This is because the more contingency you have in the plan, the greater the likelihood that your prediction will come true.

And how much contingency should you have in your plan? The answer is – as much as you can get away with. In reality, however, what people tend to put in (and manage to keep in) their plan tends to be in the order of 10–15% of the project schedule, project budget or estimated total work.

Finally, *how* do you put contingency in the plan? Are there all sorts of ways? Well basically, there are four ways corresponding to the four factors talked about in the last chapter:

> ▶ **What** the project is delivering (the goal of the project – what's in the box).
> ▶ **When** the project will be done.
> ▶ **Work** – the amount of work (person-days) in the project (which in turn can lead you to the budget).

▶ **Quality** – there are a whole bunch of jobs in the project which are about ensuring that what is done isn't just on time and within budget, but is good.

From these here are just two ways that you can put contingency in your plan. This is not because they're the only two ways, but they're two ways that are fairly widely known, they're simple and they're effective. They work well separately and together. They're in the next two sections.

CONTINGENCY USING WHAT THE PROJECT IS DELIVERING

It's true to say that some projects can be described as all or nothing projects. The great day comes, you pull the big lever and whatever it is all lights up, working perfectly. Or you pull the big lever, there's a puff of black smoke and nothing happens. The changeover to the Euro, in those countries that did it, was such a project. So too was the year 2000 project. But such projects are clearly massively high risk because if you get to the big day and you're not finished, what do you do then?

So if you can avoid this situation, you'll be far better off. If you can give the stakeholders a bit and then a bit more and then a bit more, that will work better for everybody – for these reasons:

▶ You start to solve – early on – some of the problems the project was meant to solve and the stakeholders start to get some of its benefits.

▶ The stakeholders get their hands on the solution early. They can try it out, find errors in it or ask for changes to it.

▶ The risk of failure is hugely reduced.

▶ It can ease the pressure to deliver on the project manager and the project team.

Traditionally the easiest way to do this is with the idea of 'have-to-have' and 'nice-to-have'. If you can identify the core set of things, which if you could get them to the stakeholders, would get them started, then you can plan to deliver these first and roll the rest out later.

Have-to-have and nice-to-have implies two deliveries / releases / iterations to the stakeholders, but you can have as many as you like. You could have, for example, four iterations:

▶ Iteration 1 – Have-to-have.

▶ Iteration 2 – Very important.

▶ Iteration 3 – Pretty important.

▶ Iteration 4 – Cosmetic.

Promise iteration 2 by a certain date and deliver iteration 3 and the stakeholders will love you to death. 'Under promise and over deliver', the saying goes. It doesn't quite work the other way round if you promise iteration 3 and only deliver iteration 2. However it's still better than the situation where you promise everything and deliver nothing.

Stakeholders love the idea of iterative delivery. They *hate* the big-bang approach. It terrifies the life out of them because you basically say to the stakeholders, 'Hey stakeholders, the team and I are going to be disappearing now and you're not going to see us for a long time. But when next you do, it's going to be great!' This scares the stakeholders senseless.

Many people don't see this as putting contingency in the plan at all. They just see it as good project management practice, which it is. But it is also a way of putting contingency explicitly in the plan and it's the one example of explicit contingency that stakeholders won't object to. As stated already, they really like it.

Not every project lends itself to this idea of iterative delivery. There are occasional projects that *are* all-or-nothing projects, but they are the exception. Most projects can be treated as just described and will be the better for it. So when you establish what the goal of the project is – what's in the box – then see if you can deliver this to the stakeholders in some kind of phased or iterative way.

A (slightly unusual) example of this would be the following. Say you work for a charity and your project is to set up three facilities (say, drop-in centres) for them in three different cities. You could start all three projects together and run them in parallel. But a permanent problem in the not-for-profit sector – and so, a permanent risk to the project – is that of budget cuts. What if you had the three projects rolling along and then suddenly there was a budget cut? All three would have failed.

So an alternative strategy would be to do the following. While there might be some things like planning permissions, which had long lead times, that you would do on all three projects, you would focus the bulk of your effort, energy and funding into one project to try to get it over the line. Then, if the funding was cut, at least part of the

HOW YOU NEED TO DO IT
Using the 'What' Parameter

1. Examine (with your stakeholders) whether your project has to be delivered in one big bang or can be done in a series of phases / iterations / deliveries.
2. If it can be done as a series of iterations, work with your stakeholders to identify what will go into each iteration.
3. Then revamp your plan accordingly.

solution would be in place, as opposed to the previous scenario where none of the problem would have been solved.

Iterative or phased delivery – a good thing and a good way to put contingency in your plan.

CONTINGENCY USING 'WHEN'

If you've ever allowed yourself some extra time to get to the airport, then you'll be familiar with this one. Let's say that the plan (without the contingency added) starts on January 1 and finishes on August 10. Then you tell the stakeholders it'll be done on say, August 31 and the three weeks between August 10 and August 31 becomes your contingency.

There is the question of what you tell the team. There are two schools of thought on this. One is that you don't tell them about the August 31 date. What is likely to happen in this situation though is that they'll find out; people always do.

The better approach is to do a little speech to the team that goes like this. 'Team, here's the deal. On this project I'm going to agree a delivery date of August 31 with the stakeholders. However, we have to be done by August 10. The time between August 10 and August 31 is there for contingency. If we get to August 10 and we're done, we

can go to the beach for the next three weeks. If we get
to August 10 and we're not done, this extra time that I'm
going to negotiate may save ours skin.'

After that if anybody mentions August 31, you've got to
give them a slap (not literally!) because the danger is that
people start to think in terms of August 31 and then the
contingency sort of evaporates.

This approach has many advantages. It is simple, elegant,
very visual – which is useful when you come to track the
project. However, it has one huge disadvantage. The
three weeks in a great big lump at the end of the project
draws huge attention to itself. It stands out like a sore
thumb. And almost invariably you could imagine some
stakeholder asking you to take out the contingency and
have the thing done by August 10.

If you feel that's what's going to happen to you then you
can hide the contingency. You would do this – in this
example – by slicing up the three weeks and putting little
pieces of contingency into say, each of the big pieces of
the project. These smaller pieces of contingency become
a less juicy target for the stakeholders.

But if you felt that still wouldn't be enough, that the
stakeholders would still try to remove the contingency,
then you could do the following. Call the contingency
something else. Things like 'Finalise' or 'Complete documentation' or 'Housekeeping' or 'wrap-up' are all
possibilities. Or you can use techno babble if you're in

HOW YOU NEED TO DO IT
Using the 'When' Parameter

1. Take the duration of your entire project as determined by your plan so far.
2. Calculate 15% of that duration and add it on to the end of your project. This is your contingency.
3. If you are happy that the stakeholders won't try to remove this, then tell the team the date they date they must work to (the date from number 1) and tell the stakeholders the date that you are committing to (the date from number 2).
4. If, on the other hand, you believe that the stakeholders will try to remove the contingency then slice this period of time up and put a little piece of it into each of the big phases of your project.
5. If you still believe that the stakeholders will target these small pieces of contingency, then give them a different name other than 'contingency'.

113

a business that has a lot of jargon. So, if it was a software project, you could call the contingency something like 'Update object-oriented table vectors' or something like that. Just be sure to have another piece of techno babble ready in case anyone asks what 'Update object-oriented table vectors' actually is!

One final point then is that this and the phased delivery approach to contingency work well together. So, for example, you could have say, three iterations and within each iteration, you could have:

▶ First date – this is what the team will aim for.
▶ Later date – this is what is what you'll promise the stakeholders.

WHO SAID IT

"If you don't actively attack the risks on your project, then the risks will actively attack you."
– Tom Gilb

RISK ANALYSIS

The other aspect of strengthening your project plan is to do a risk analysis on the project, i.e. to try to identify the major threats to the project and to see what, if anything, you can do to reduce or eliminate these threats. Here's how to do that.

First of all, you want to involve the team, just as you did when you were doing the estimating. Brainstorm with them and try to come up with all of the risks to the project that you can think of. Risks are the things that could cause the project to get into trouble or derail it.

Next, you want to assess each of these risks in terms of its likelihood (L) – the probability of its happening. You can use different scales – 1–10, 1–5, 1–3. The example below uses a three point scale – 3 = high (very likely to happen), 2 = medium, 1 = low (not very likely to happen).

After that, you want to assess – again for each risk – the impact (I) if it were to happen. Use the same scale as for the likelihood. Thus, a three-point scale would be – 3 = high (has a big effect if it happens), 2 = medium, 1 = low (doesn't have much of an effect if it happens).

Multiplying the likelihood (L) by the impact (I) gives you your Exposure (E) to that particular risk – how open you are to that risk. The larger the number the greater the exposure.

Brainstorm what action(s) you can take to reduce or eliminate that risk. The result of this will almost certainly be some additional jobs that must then be put back into the plan – in the list of jobs and processed from there i.e. effort estimated, dependencies established, people identified to do them. This will in turn affect the project management effort calculation.

And one last point. Do the risk analysis regularly – every week or couple of weeks. Risks that you took action against will reduce in severity or disappear altogether. New risks will emerge as the project unfolds. Doing the risk analysis regularly is a way of looking ahead trying to anticipate problems and do something about them before they become serious.

Let's just take one example of a risk and how to deal with it. In many organisations, a fairly standard risk to most projects is that you are given people to work on your project, but then a new project or some emergency crops up and your people are taken to deal with that other thing. So there's the risk – 'Lose people to another project'.

Likelihood? In most organisations, this is fairly high, so grade it 3. Impact? Well, it's big. If you lose people, you lose supply and so your supply – demand equation goes out of balance, so another 3. This gives an Exposure – multiplying the Likelihood by the Impact – of 9.

HOW YOU NEED TO DO IT
Risk Analysis

1. Identify with your team the risks to the project.
2. For each risk, grade it in terms of the likelihood (L).
3. For each risk, grade it in terms of, if it were to happen, what its impact (I) would be.
4. Multiply the Likelihood (2) by the Impact (3) to give your Exposure (E) to that particular risk.
5. For each risk with a high exposure (an exposure of 6 or 9), identify what action(s) you can take to reduce or eliminate that risk and put these actions into your plan.
6. Do the risk analysis every week or couple of weeks.

And what action can you take to deal with this? Easy – it's change control. Remember that change control is making the right choice between your three options of:

▶ It's a big change
▶ Use the contingency
▶ Suck it up.

So the right choice here is the first option. Losing people from your project is a big change and nothing else. Your boss or your stakeholders have every right to take the people. But then you are completely within your rights to tell them what the effect of this will be. So the action will be that if you lose your people to another project, you will revise your plan and tell the stakeholders what they can now expect. (There's more on this in the next chapter.)

After you've put the contingency into your plan and done a risk analysis, you're at last ready to deal with the constraints. Just before that though, here's something. It's called 'how to assess a project in five minutes'. Sounds useful, doesn't it?

ASSESSING A PROJECT IN FIVE MINUTES

If you've ever watched TV dramas about hospital emergency rooms, like 'ER' or 'Holby City', you'll be familiar with that scene where the crash cart comes through the door, there's some misfortunate person lying on it and the A & E doctor does some quick checks on the patient. What the doctor is looking for are the patient's 'vital signs'. There are a handful of things – body temperature, pulse, blood pressure and respiratory rate, pain and pupil size – which can give the doctor a rapid indication of the state of the patient's heath.

Just as people have vital signs, projects have vital signs. There are a handful of things which the presence or absence of them can give a rapid indication of the state of the project. This may seem to you to be a very simple tool. It is. It is also immensely powerful. One client of mine has used it on all sorts of personal and work-related projects. He describes it as 'the gift that keeps giving and giving'. You will find this useful in any of the following situations:

▶ You are asked to take over a project that is already running.
▶ You are asked to assess a project.
▶ Somebody who reports to you is running a project – how do you know if the project is in good shape?
▶ In project status meetings – the measurement you do here essentially provides the agenda for the meeting.
▶ A sub-contractor does a presentation of their project plan. How do you know whether it is a good plan or not?

The tool for measuring a project's vital signs is called a Probability of Success Indicator or PSI. The PSI is a measurement you can take at any point in a project's life and it tells you how likely or not the project is to succeed. If used at the beginning of a project, it becomes a practical approach/checklist to gauge the probability of success before a project begins. Thus, it can stop turkey projects from getting off the ground. At any time, it will tell you if a project is viable or not, and identify the warning signs that the project is destined to fail.

The PSI is described in the next section and just to keep the discussion as practical as possible, imagine you've been handed the following project. A project which is scheduled to take 17 months has been running for 11. There are about 250 people working on it. The project is very significant to the organisation and so a very senior person has been given the job of running it. There is lots of activity on the project. People are working long hours. Is the project in good shape or not?

MEASURING THE PSI

The PSI is measured by rating the project against the following criteria. (For each criterion a maximum score is given).

1. **How well-defined or not is the goal? (20)** The acid test here is that if you were to ask each stakeholder what the goal of the project is, and if each were to give you almost exactly the same

reply, then the goal is well-defined. Otherwise it is not. You only get a 20 when the project is complete because only then do you know exactly what was achieved. A project which is at a very early stage and where the goal has yet to be nailed down, would score low. A project where the goal had been reasonably well clarified, but agreement is still needed from some of the stakeholders would get a medium/in-the-middle sort of score. Pick a number between 0 and 20. In the example previously described, you discover that specifications for some of the project still don't exist even though the project is due to end in 6 months. Based on the proportion of specifications completed to those still not done, you score the project 14.

2. **Is there a final, definitive detailed list of jobs where every one has been broken down to the 1–5 day level of detail? (20)** Zero is no list. You might get 2 or 3 for a high level Work Breakdown Structure i.e. just the big pieces of work in the project. You only get 20 when the project completes because only then do you know exactly what the list of jobs was. Pick a number between 0 and 20. If the goal (Step 1) scores low, then this will score low, since – if you won't know what you're trying to do, how could you have a list of jobs to do it? In the example, some parts of the project have plans, some parts have no plans. The bits that haven't been specified could have no plans (that are based in reality, at any

rate). Since only 70% (14/20) of the project is defined, this is the most that this could score. A 70% would be possible if all of the bits of the project that were specified had plans. However, some don't. Score this 10.

3. **Does the project have somebody who, day-to-day, shepherds all of the jobs forward? (10)** If the leader can be named and that person has adequate time available to run the project, then give 10, otherwise give 0. In the example, the very senior person still has all their other responsibilities – in fact, it turns out they have a full-time job – so they can't give anywhere near enough time to devote to a project of this magnitude. In addition, they see the day-to-day shepherding of the project as work that is really beneath them. This project doesn't have a leader. It has somebody with the title but nobody doing the job. Score 0.

4. **Are there people to do all of the jobs identified in 2 and do those people have enough time availability to devote to the project? (10)** Essentially you are checking here whether there is enough supply to match demand. If there aren't any/enough people to do the work, score this 0 or low. Also take into account that this step should be in the same proportion as Step 2 e.g. a 14/20 for Step 2 would give at most a 7/10 for Step 4. There are lots of people – 250, we said in this example. The problem is that we don't fully know yet (because of 1 and 2) what

the people should be working on. Is there adequate supply to match demand? We don't know because we don't know what the demand is. Since only 50% (10/20) of the jobs are identified, this could score no more than 50%. Give it 5.

5. **Is there contingency in the plan? (10)** The more contingency, the higher the score out of 5. In the example, there really isn't a plan ('it's a plan, Jim but not as we know it'), so score 0.

6. **Has an up-to-date risk analysis been done and are the jobs to reduce those risks part of the project plan? (5)** This 5 is for how well or badly the risk reducing activities have been identified and are being carried out. For a project with lots of level 6 and level 9 risks (i.e. a high-risk project) score low; for projects with few 9's and

WHO SAID IT

"The major difference between a thing that might go wrong and a thing that cannot possibly go wrong is that when a thing that cannot possibly go wrong goes wrong it usually turns out to be impossible to get at or repair."
– Douglas Adams

6's (i.e. a low-risk project), score high. In the example it turns out that there's no risk analysis available, so score 0.

This example gives a total score of 29. Let's move on to see what this means.

INTERPRETING PSI SCORES

If the Goal Isn't Right, Nothing Will Be Right

If the goal isn't right, you miss one of the two opportunities to get a high score, but notice now, how it all unravels. If you don't know what you're trying to do, creating a list of jobs to do it is impossible. (So too, it's worth noting, is setting the expectations of the stakeholders. If you don't know what you're trying to do, how could you set them? What will happen then is that everyone will set his or her own expectations.) Thus the list is flawed resulting in missing the other opportunity to get a high score. If the list is flawed then running the project (number 3) is impossible, as is assigning people to the jobs (number 4). Contingency (number 5) and risk analysis (number 6) will have no meaning.

You can see that this explains why projects whose goal is vague *never* succeed. It's not that they rarely succeed or are unlikely to succeed. They *can't* succeed. So if, in the future, you find yourself working on such a project, either get it sorted out or else go do something useful with your life. Learn to windsurf or play the piano or go work for a charity because the project will not succeed with a vague goal.

40 Is an Important Threshold

A PSI should start off low and rise steadily over the life of the project. Initially projects may not score more than 40, and this can just mean that there is more work to be done in terms of scoping the project (1) and planning it (2 through 6). However, a project should quickly go above 40 and stay above it. (Notice that the latter isn't guaranteed, and a project can drop back again. This could happen, for example, if a major change to the scope of the project went uncontrolled.)

Low Scores Always Point You at the Priority Problem Areas

Low scores are a bit like yellow warning lights on the dashboard of a car. They tell you that of all the things you could be doing on this project, fixing the things that need to be fixed, so that your scores go up, so that you extinguish the warning lights, are the most important.

You Can Do Anything You Like on a Poorly Planned Project and It Won't Make the Blindest Bit of Difference

There is a thing in project management called Brooks' Law. It says that 'adding people to a late project makes it later.' The above statement – 'you can do anything you like ...' – can be viewed as a generalization of Brooks' Law. It basically says that if your project gets into difficulties, go back and look at the plan; don't just, for example, blindly ask everyone to work harder. The problem is in the plan, not in the execution of the plan.

So how would you interpret the previous example where the project is two-thirds of the way through its planned life with a PSI well below 40? Well clearly, this project is in disastrous shape and is going nowhere. It has no chance of succeeding in its current form and will seriously overshoot its budget and its deadline.

To rescue this project, the following would need to be done:

1. Re-plan the project. (By including contingency in the plan and doing a risk analysis, scores 5 and 6 will both climb.)
2. Use the plan to reset the expectations of the stakeholders. (This will not be a pleasant exercise.)

126

HOW YOU NEED TO DO IT
Calculating the PSI

If you're trying to very quickly understand the health or status of a project, do the following:

1. Score it against the six criteria previously described.
2. Add up the six scores to give a total.
3. If the project is at an early stage in its life and the total is below 40, there's no problem. The low individual scores remind you where to focus your efforts.
4. If the project is at an advanced stage and the total is below 40, be very, very afraid. Happily, however, the low scores will point you at the issues that need to be addressed. Take the actions to address these issues as a matter of urgency.
5. Record the scores in Excel and repeat this exercise a week later. You could also draw a little graph which should show the PSI rising as the project proceeds.

3. Complete the specifications. This will cause the 14/20 score to climb.
4. With the goal specified it will be possible to finalise the detailed list of jobs (causing the 10/20 to climb).

Now people will be working on the right things and everything else should start falling into place.

WHAT YOU NEED TO READ

▶ The 'Risk Analysis Techniques' article by Geoffrey H. Wold and Robert F. Shriver in *The Disaster Recovery Journal* (www.drj.com/new2dr/w3_030.htm) has a good exloration of risk.

▶ *Brilliant Project Management: What the Best Project Managers Know, Say and Do* by Stephen Barker and Rob Cole (Prentice Hall, 2007) would be a good general next step in exploring project management further.

▶ *The Survivor's Club: The Secrets and Science That Could Save Your Life* by Ben Sherwood (Michael Joseph, 2009) is a book about disasters and how to survive them. While hopefully, your project management career won't land you in life threatening situations, there's a lot to be learnt here about resilience, coping with stress, adversity and bouncing back.

▶ *Waltzing with Bears: Managing Risk on Software Projects* by Tom DeMarco and Timothy Lister (Dorset House Publishing, 2003) has lots of useful ideas, techniques and tools that are applicable way beyond software projects.

IF YOU ONLY REMEMBER ONE THING

If something can go wrong, it will.
Murphy's Law

CHAPTER 5

MANAGING EXPECTATIONS

WHATS IT'S ALL ABOUT ▶

▶ How to make commitments to stakeholders

▶ Working out your options using the 'what', 'when', 'work' and 'quality' factors

▶ Negotiation using the facts

▶ How to deal with impossible missions

▶ What happens when you say yes to impossible missions

▶ A variety of ways for shortening projects

MAKING COMMITMENTS TO STAKEHOLDERS

Okay, so you've got your robust, toughened-up plan for your project. You're now ready to go and deal with the constraints.

The first possibility then is that there are no conflicts between the plan and the constraints. For example, let's say they've told you that the project has to be done:

- ▶ by September 30;
- ▶ for a budget of $100k;
- ▶ and you can't hire any more people;

and lo and behold, your plan says that the project can be done:

- ▶ by September 30;
- ▶ for a budget of say, $98.5k;
- ▶ and it's possible to do it with your existing team.

Well, this is a happy day indeed. You have a robust plan. It has all the good things in it that have been talked about:

- ▶ a clear goal;
- ▶ lots of detail used to make the estimates;
- ▶ supply matched to demand;
- ▶ contingency to take care of bad things that will inevitably happen;
- ▶ risk analysis to try and stop some of those bad things from happening.

You can look your stakeholders in the eye and say, 'Yep, we can do that' and then proceed to execute your plan as will be described in Chapter 6.

The only problem with that rosy little scenario, of course, is that it just doesn't happen very often. And generally, what's more likely is that what the plan says is possible and what the constraints say is necessary, are not the same. So say, for instance, same constraints as above:

- ► by September 30;
- ► for a budget of $100k;
- ► and you can't hire any more people.

But your plan says the project will:

- ► take until October 22;
- ► require a budget of $121k;
- ► and need say, two extra people.

What do you do now?

The answer to that question is that you do exactly what the mechanic in the garage, the doctor in the surgery, the plumber who comes to your house or any other sensible professional does. You come up with options. You identify different ways in which the project could be done. Sure, the stakeholders have their constraints, their wishes. But when do people ever get everything that they wish for? The stakeholders have their constraints. Now you're going to tell them what's possible and what's not possible.

COMING UP WITH OPTIONS

You can think of the original plan you came up with as the vanilla plan. If the stakeholders don't like vanilla, that's no problem. You can come up with plenty of other flavours – raspberry, rum and raisin, strawberry. Not only that, your plan is a flavour generator. It can come up with all kinds of flavours. The stakeholders can ask you, for example, whether it can make banana with a hint of pistachio and you can see whether you can make that particular flavour. It's perhaps worth mentioning too that your plan, your flavour generator, isn't infinitely variable. In other words, there are certain flavours it *can't* make – but more of this anon.

Here first, is how to generate the flavours, the options, the alternative plans. It's done by using the same four things that one keeps running into in project management. Once again, they are:

> ▶ **What** the project is delivering.
> ▶ **When** the project will be done.
> ▶ **Work** – the amount of work (person-days) in the project.
> ▶ **Quality** – there are a whole bunch of jobs in the project which are about ensuring that what is done isn't just on time and within budget, but is good.

Here is their use in turn. Notice too as you read through the next four sections that the methods described under

134

each parameter can be used singly or in combination with one another.

Options Using the 'What' Factor

In trying to come up a version of the plan that will be acceptable to the stakeholders, the first thing you can look at is whether you can reduce the scope of the project in some way. Here are the possibilities:

▶ Can you give them a slimmed down version of the project by the date they required or for the budget they gave you? You can say things like, 'For that budget, here's what we can do. Give us a bit more money and we can do these extra things.'

▶ Or can you do some kind of phased or incremental delivery as described in the previous chapter? Could you give them the have-to-haves by the date they required or for the budget they gave you?

Just by using this one factor, the 'what' factor, you can see there are rich possibilities for coming up with versions of the plan that could be acceptable to the stakeholders. And all you need is one. Once you've found one that they're prepared to accept then you're in business.

But there are lots of other possibilities with the other factors. Here's the 'when' factor next.

Options Using the 'When' Factor

The 'when' factor is one that's not often looked at when it comes to coming up with alternative plans and it's a pity because it too has rich possibilities.

There is a tendency to treat constraint dates – 'it has to be done by *this* date' – as though they were handed down from God. And some dates *are* like that. The changeover to the euro, the year 2000 problem, changes to say, tax regimes made by governments, sporting events, are all examples of projects that bring with them a 'hard' constraint, a hard deadline that can't be moved.

But there are many dates that are *not* hard dates. They were merely chosen arbitrarily by some boss or stake-holder. So don't fall into the trap of thinking that all deadlines that you are given are hard and can't be changed. Some certainly are and can't. But many aren't – and it's always worth checking. Here are some things to look out for:

▶ Dates around Christmas like December 20 or December 31 or people saying 'before the end of the year'. If you deliver the project to them at a time like that, will they actually be able to do anything with it? Maybe they will but maybe they'll be so busy with business as usual or year-end type stuff, that realistically it'll be the new year before they can get round to doing anything with it. Great – that gives you further possibilities and options.

▶ Does the date they've given you as the deadline fall on a Saturday, a Sunday or a public holiday? If it does, there's a good chance they haven't thought it out properly and there's some 'wiggle room' in the date.

▶ If the date they've given you is phrased vaguely, for example, 'by the end of October' as opposed to them saying 'by October 31', then it may mean there's some flexibility in it.

▶ There are some cultures / countries where some dates are decidedly dubious. August in France – everybody's in traffic jams trying to get to the beach; July in Sweden are examples.

▶ And finally, you may be the victim of a sort of reverse contingency, where they don't actually want it until a later date, but they've told you an earlier date, so that if you slip, they won't be delayed.

So don't take the date they've given you as gospel. It may be – but also, it may not be. And, if it's not, then that gives you further options to explore.

Options Using the 'Work' Factor

The possibility here is to add more people. Be a little bit careful with this one. Chapter 4 mentioned briefly Brooks' Law – 'adding people to a late project makes it later'. More generally, adding people to a project (i.e. increasing the supply, the amount of work available) won't necessarily speed a project up. While this may sound counter-intuitive, if you think about it, you can see why this would be so.

Because what happens if you add more people to a project? Well, you have to find these people, hire or assign them, bring them on board, they have a learning curve, they take time away from people already working on the project, you have to train them, bring them up to speed, they require hand-holding and nurturing. And it may be that by the time you've factored in all of these things, adding people to your project:

- ▶ will have little effect;
- ▶ will have no effect;
- ▶ could actually slow it down.

So be careful when somebody says to you, 'I'll give you whatever resources you need to get the job done'. Extra resources may not help. (This is the familiar, 'If it takes one woman nine months to have a baby, can nine women have one in a month?' effect.)

And having said all that, there may be times when adding more people definitely would help. Maybe you can hire people with specialist skills who can hit the ground running and require very little learning curve. Or maybe the work to be done isn't that skilled so that more warm bodies would make a difference.

Either way, there may or may not be further options, possibilities and ways that the project could be done to the satisfaction of the stakeholders. And notice too that you don't have to bring the extra people onto the project and see what happens. Rather, you can add the extra tasks involved in bringing in these extra people into your plan and see if it will have a beneficial effect. See – the plan really *is* a simulator of the project.

Options Using the 'Quality' Factor

Finally yes, of course you never compromise on quality (!), but there may be things you can do under this heading. Specifically:

Can you shorten review or approval cycles?

A lot of time on projects gets spent hanging around while you wait for people (bosses or stakeholders) to review say, documents or approve things or make decisions. Ask the stakeholders if they can speed these up. Show them that they too have a part to play in coming up with a version of the plan that will work for both them, but also for you as the project manager. This is nice from you in that it shows the stakeholders that the resolution of the constraints is not just your problem but their problem too.

NEGOTIATION USING THE FACTS

And so between these four factors, it is possible to come up with a whole set of possible ways that the project could be done. You then offer these to the stakeholders and they pick one. Job done!

Notice that it doesn't matter if the stakeholders are more senior than you, more powerful than you, higher up in the staff structure than you, more assertive/aggressive/bullying than you. When the negotiation is carried out using the facts in the plan – the estimates that you've gone to such trouble to produce – then you can't lose.

And furthermore, your power, your authority comes from the fact that you know more about this project than anybody else on the planet. You are – quite literally – the world's walking expert on this project, so use that authority wisely. In particular, don't let people steamroll or browbeat you into agreeing something that you really oughtn't.

What can you expect to happen if you begin to use 'negotiation using the facts'? In the past your stakeholders may have been used to you agreeing to everything – to always saying 'sure'. Now suddenly, you're not doing that. Will they say that they're delighted you've found a better way to manage their projects? Unlikely. Here's what will happen and here's how to respond to it.

The first thing they will do is to question your estimates. They'll want to know why the numbers are the way they are. How did you calculate the supply and demand? And you'd better be sure you've done the calculations right, because if you haven't you'll be sent away with a flea in your ear. And rightly so! So make sure the sums are correct.

And don't see them questioning the sums as any kind of personal attack on you. Okay, there are psychopathic bosses and stakeholders out there, but they're something of a rarity. Most bosses and stakeholders are just exactly like you – under pressure, trying to do too much with too little, under pressure to take on impossible missions from *their* bosses. So in questioning your estimates, they're not attacking you – they're just doing their job.

Assuming that your numbers are correct, the second thing they will do is start to push. Again this is not a personal attack on you; again, they're just doing their job. They will push in the sense that they will try to get you to improve on what you're offering. So say, for example, you've said that the best you can do (the best option that you can offer them) is to have the project ready by 18 January 2011 – say from a 1 July 2010 start. They will almost certainly ask if you could have it done before Christmas or before the end of the year.

So you'd better have an answer ready. Because if you give way a little, they'll push some more. And if you give way again? Well, you can see where that could lead. You could be gently coaxed into accepting the impossible mission after all. So, know, going into the negotiation, where you're going to draw the line – where you're going to say, 'thus far and no further'. Even better, maybe have something you're prepared to give away. Your boss will feel like he's had a successful negotiation (that he's won) and you'll still have a project that lies in the realm of the possible.

WHO SAID IT

"When the facts are at hand, what's the need for words?"
– Sallust

Remember that bosses and stakeholders aren't entitled to expect miracles. If they do, it's only because you've given them miracles in the past – you've accepted impossible missions. But bosses and stakeholders *are* entitled to know how they stand – they're entitled to honesty – and to commitments (from you) which have some chance of succeeding.

IMPOSSIBLE MISSIONS AND HOW TO DEAL WITH THEM

The foregoing should really be the end of this discussion. You build your plan. If the stakeholders aren't happy with that, you come up with a bunch of options – other ways the project could be done. The stakeholders accept one of those and that's that.

However, this chapter wouldn't be complete if it didn't talk about one other issue that arises when you're trying to set the expectations of the stakeholders. This is when the stakeholders won't accept any of your options. Furthermore, they keep insisting on an option that your plan says is impossible. In other words, they're trying to force you to take on an impossible mission.

An impossible mission is a version of the project that your plan says is impossible to achieve. Another way to think about an impossible mission is that it is a supply-demand imbalance. There is too much demand (work to be done)

143

and not enough supply (people to do the work), but the stakeholders don't care. They want it done anyway.

It has to be said that – sometimes – impossible missions come packaged in some very unpleasant stuff. Things like 'don't bring me problems, bring me solutions', 'if you don't do it, I'll find somebody who will', 'you're being inflexible', 'you're not being a team player', 'we have no choice – we have to do it', 'that's not the kind of attitude we want around here', 'we want can-do people here', 'I don't think you're suited to the culture of this organisation', JFDI (where J stands for 'just', D for 'do' and I for 'it') and so on. Maybe you've come across such things yourself.

Sometimes – it has to be said – the pressure to take on an impossible mission can come entirely from ourselves. You want to show your boss, your peers, your team, your stakeholders that you're good guy [gal] and that you have the right stuff. Then, all the boss has to say is something like, 'this is a very aggressive deadline but we know you're the man [woman] for the job', and – with almost no pressure from anybody – you're there, saying, 'okay'.

However it comes packaged, whatever your motivation, if you get handed an impossible mission, what should you do?

The correct and only answer to the question is that you should say 'no' to it. By which is meant, you should say

144

'no' using the facts. You should do exactly what was described above – identify a bunch of options that are achievable and allow them to pick one. You should do this even if you have to drag them kicking and screaming to the negotiation. Remember that you are the one with the authority. You know more about the project than anybody else.

Now you may be saying to yourself at this point that you couldn't possibly imagine yourself saying 'no' to an impossible mission – to bosses or stakeholders. So let's explore that a bit more. Let's see what happens if you say yes to impossible missions.

WHAT HAPPENS WHEN YOU SAY YES TO IMPOSSIBLE MISSIONS

If you say yes to impossible missions then you join a very select group of people in your organisation that you can think of as the 'magicians'. Magicians do exactly as the name suggests – they do magic tricks. They take seemingly impossible supply-demand imbalances and – somehow – make them succeed.

If an organisation has magicians working for it, it should love them. It should give them salary rises, stock options, profit sharing, company cars, big bonuses, flowers on their birthday and presents at Christmas. This is because magicians do an extraordinary thing. Imagine you went to a job interview and the person behind the desk said, 'what do you do?' If you said, 'I do impossible missions', her immediate response would be, 'sign here, how much do we have to pay you?'

But there is a problem with being a magician that has to be talked about. To illustrate it picture a theatre. In the front row of the theatre are your stakeholders. There's your team, your boss, your boss's boss, your other stakeholders. Now you come out on stage and, right before their eyes, you do the first basic trick. You pull a rabbit from the hat. In other words, you take a mission of small impossibility (i.e. a small supply-demand imbalance) and you make it happen.

It's a sweet moment. The stakeholders are impressed. Your team are saying, 'He led us to victory'. Your boss is nudging your boss's boss and saying, 'I hired her'. Your stakeholders are applauding. You and your team put in a big effort, worked night and weekends and it all paid off.

But now your problems begin because the next time you go on stage, pulling a rabbit from the hat isn't going to impress anybody. So you're going to have to do a more impressive trick – a bigger animal to be pulled from the hat. So you move on to little dogs – a little terrier, then a medium-sized dog like a German Shepherd, then a very big dog like an Irish Wolfhound. After that mules, donkeys, ponies, horses, hippopotamuses, rhinoceroses, elephants, bigger and bigger animals being pulled from the hat – bigger and bigger supply demand imbalances.

Once you got up into these big animals, it's worth pointing out a few interesting things. The first one is that you start to get the feeling that you're invincible, that you've cracked it, that you've figured out how to do these supply-demand imbalances. You have a feeling of bring it on, that you can deal with it.

The second thing that happens is that things aren't quite as rosy as they were when you were doing the smaller animals, the smaller supply-demand imbalances. Your team are either burnt out or on the way to being burnt out. Why is this? Well, it's because just as with regular magicians, there's no magic, there's a trick. There's also a trick here. You have a trick for closing the supply demand imbalances. What is it? Where do you find the extra supply from to close the gap? Hey, you just get everybody to work longer hours, to suck it up. It's a pretty lousy trick really.

So your team are exhausted. Your boss and your boss's boss are wondering why morale is low or staff turnover is high. Your stakeholders are probably still happy enough although maybe they've seen some close shaves on projects just recently as these big supply-demand imbalances looked in doubt right up to the end.

And finally, there are some stakeholders that haven't really been mentioned up until now. You can picture them sitting in the second row of the theatre. These are people like wives, husbands, girlfriends, boyfriends, partners, housemates, mothers, fathers, brothers, sisters, cats, dogs – those that love us and like to spend time with us. But they get to spend no time with us when we're doing these big impossible missions because we're either at work, thinking about work, bringing work home with us, calling up and saying, 'I won't be home until late' or cancelling things you planned to do together or saying, 'I can't take my holidays during the project'.

Stay at it long enough and there will come the day when you pull the biggest mammal on earth from the hat. The blue whale is the world's biggest living mammal and weighs 150 tonnes, so you pull that from the hat. You'd like to think that at that point you could stop. You would have reached the pinnacle of your project management career. Essentially – they would let you retire. They would give you an office with a view, a large compensation package and basically you wouldn't have to do very much. You'd become a sort of company treasure and your main purpose would be to teach other, younger magicians how to pull blue whales from hats.

But of course, you know that's not what's going to happen. After you pull the blue whale from the hat, the stakeholders will merely say, 'Okay, whaddya gonna do now?' Given that there is no bigger mammal that you can pull from the hat, you're going to have to find a different trick. So there's trick called sawing the lady in half. You start doing that. The stakeholders are blown away. They knew you were good with mammals from hats; they can't believe you can saw ladies in half.

Except that one night you go on stage, the lady gets in the box, you pull the ripcord on the chainsaw and as you begin sawing, fountains of blood start spurting out.

Because this is the problem with being a magician. Sooner or later you take on a supply-demand imbalance that can't actually be resolved. (After all, there's a limit to the supply. There are only seven days in a week, twenty four hours in a day.)

And when this happens, it's a very bad moment. Your team are devastated. They put in a huge effort for nothing – their name is mud. Your management are wondering how it all went so horribly wrong. The rest of the stake-holders are saying, 'What do we do now?' It's awful.

And usually what the magician does at that point is that he slinks quietly away. If it's a big organisation maybe he can find a place where they haven't heard about him. More likely he'll go to some new organisation where his fame hasn't preceded him. And what will he do here? Will he have learned anything from the terrible things that happened?

Nope – he will not. Instead, he'll start doing low-grade tricks again. Little furry animals, small dogs and he'll proceed back up the same dreadful escalator another time.

This is the problem with being a magician. This is the problem with saying yes to impossible missions. It's unsustainable. Or to put it more bluntly: You work harder and harder, your team work harder and harder. You have a temporary feeling of invincibility while in fact you're hurtling towards a cliff. And sooner or later, you go off the edge and really screw something up. Could anything be more unattractive?

HOW YOU NEED TO DO IT
Selling Your Plan to the Stakeholders

1. Having built your plan, see if it will satisfy the stakeholders' constraints. If it will, job done.
2. If it won't, come up with flavours of the plan – other ways the project could be done – using the four factors singly or in combination.
3. Get agreement from the stakeholders on one of these as the way the project will be done. Job done.
4. Never agree to an impossible mission. Always do number 3 instead.

WHO SAID IT

"The hen is the wisest of all the animal creation because she never cackles until after the egg has been laid."
— **Abraham Lincoln**

SHORTENING PROJECTS

Now you know how to run any project successfully, is there anything that can usefully be added to that knowledge? Well there is. Wouldn't it be nice if you could not only run the project successfully but run it in the shortest possible time.

A lot of this chapter has been about trying to satisfy stakeholders' constraints. These constraints can range from the challenging right through to the downright impossible. As the 21st century advances, speed seems to have become the constraint that stakeholders are most exercised over. They want projects done quicker, faster, as soon as possible, in the shortest possible time.

WHO YOU NEED TO KNOW
Abraham Lincoln

Abraham Lincoln (1809–1865) was the 16th president of the United States. He stands as one of the greatest project managers for his ability to set and manage the expectations of his stakeholders and to motivate his team. Lincoln led the United States during the four terrible years of the American Civil War. This was a war fought not for territory or conquest or riches or spoils, but for an idea. That idea was that the United States would remain one nation and that this idea – by itself – was worth fighting and dying for. (The freeing of the slaves as a war objective came later in the war.) That he was able to formulate this idea and motivate men as he did was, and remains an extraordinary achievement.

You've seen already that if you are to have any chance of doing this then you must plan. A little planning is better than a lot of fire fighting. Time invested in planning will be repaid many times over by fire fighting you don't have to have to do as a result. If you've ever heard anybody say, 'We don't have time to plan – just go do it', they are invariably barking up the wrong tree and the chances are that their words will come back to haunt them.

But you can do better than just planning your projects, as already described. There are other things you can do if you wish to get them done as quickly as possible. Learn these techniques and you'll be in the top 1% of project managers.

The basic proposition is that it is possible to run projects far more quickly than is done at the moment. The obvious question then is why aren't they run like this. The answer appears to be a combination of the following factors:

1. Most project managers don't think it's actually possible. They think they're lucky if they can bring the project in on time and within budget.
2. The stakeholders don't think it's actually possible – *they* think *they're* lucky if the project comes in on time and within budget.
3. Nobody knows what getting the project done early would mean financially.
4. Projects aren't planned properly – if they're not planned properly they can't possibly be done quickly.

5. Getting projects done quickly is not in the PMI's Project Management Body of Knowledge.
6. "What's wrong with the way we do things at the moment?" syndrome.
7. People are afraid that if they try to do the project fast they'll miss something important.

And so the result of all this is that ... they don't try!

And can you see that if projects could be run more quickly, the benefits would be enormous? They would include:

▶ reduced costs and money saved;
▶ increased profits;
▶ improved revenues;
▶ improved cash flow;
▶ organisations stealing a march on their competitors;
▶ business benefits delivered quicker;
▶ the risk of the project running over would be reduced;
▶ not to mention ... increased team morale, greater job satisfaction and all that good stuff.

So what follows here then are seven techniques for getting projects done quicker. They can be used singly or in any combination on one or many projects. The only assumption is that you know how to plan (and in particular, estimate), track and report a project properly. The techniques are these:

1. Basic techniques.
2. Scope and plan a project in a day.
3. Calculate the value of getting it done early.
4. Lay the plan out as a strip board.
5. Do a Mission Briefing for the team and for the other stakeholder.
6. Make Every Day Count (8 items).
7. O'Connell's Law.

and they are discussed in turn.

1 Basic Techniques

These are the simplest and most obvious techniques of all:

▶ Ask people could they try to get something finished before the weekend, a long weekend, a holiday weekend, a public holiday, their own holidays, Christmas, Easter – irrespective of what the plan may actually say.

▶ See if you can get the time of people full time instead of part time. Somebody working full time for you for a month may well be more valuable (in terms of speeding up the project) than that same person half time for two months. You get the same amount of work (1 person-month) from them so that should make it an easy 'sell' to their boss.

▶ Can you parallel things? Or overlap things, i.e. can you actually start job B – which strictly, speaking depends on job A, before job A finishes? It might be possible. For example, you don't have to wait until all the testing of something is finished before you start fixing the errors in it.

▶ Look at the critical path as described in Chapter 2.

2 Scope and Plan a Project in a Day

Scoping and Planning a Project in a Day – Why

It is possible to scope and plan a project – even a very large one – in a day. If you don't scope and plan the project in a day, what's the alternative? It goes something like this:

1. Somebody identifies some kind of need or requirement or problem that needs to be solved.

2. Based on this somebody does some ferreting around and then writes a proposal/business case/specification.

3. This is reviewed by the stakeholders and the reviews are fed back to the author of the document.

4. There are updates to the document, plus perhaps flurries of e-mail exchanges, phone calls, requests for information and meetings to resolve various issues.
5. Items 3 and 4 get looped around a number of times until finally ...
6. There is agreement on what is going to be done.
7. Then somebody is charged with building a plan.
8. That somebody does some ferreting around and then writes a plan.
9. That plan is reviewed by some or all of the stakeholders and the reviews are fed back to the author.
10. There are updates to the plan, perhaps more e-mails, phone calls, requests for information and meetings – particularly if there is a gap between what the stakeholders want and what the project team say is possible.
11. Items 9 and 10 get looped around a number of times until finally ...
12. There is agreement on the plan.

This process can take weeks ... months ... years, in some cases.

As an alternative to all of this carry on, you can scope and plan the project in a day.

In their book, *Developing Products in Half the Time* (see 'What You Need to Read' at the end of this chapter), the authors Smith and Reinertsen refer to the beginning of the project as 'the fuzzy front end'. They say this: 'Time is an irreplaceable resource. When a month of potential development time is squandered, it can never be recovered ... each month of delay has a quantifiable cost of delay. Our goal as developers is to find opportunities to buy cycle time for less than this cost. These opportunities, large and small, appear throughout the development process. There is, however, one place that we could call the 'bargain basement' of cycle time reduction opportunities. It is the place that we consistently find the least expensive opportunities to achieve large improvements in time to market. We call this stage of development the Fuzzy Front End of the development programme. It is the fuzzy zone between when the opportunity is known and when we mount a serious effort on the development project.'

If the 'fuzzy front end' is where 'opportunities to achieve large improvements in time to market' are greatest, then scoping and planning a project in a day is way of maxing out those opportunities.

Projects can often be very start-stop in nature. We do some stuff and then we have to wait, for example, for reviews, or approval or for input from other people. Nowhere is this truer than in the fuzzy front end. Everyone believes they have something to contribute, lots of people want 'signoff', and there are always those who feel that their input is being ignored. At the same time, because the project hasn't really yet gotten off the ground, there are always a million and one things more immediate and pressing. The net result of all of this can be a long and frustrating period while requirements are identified, nailed down and agreed. You can circumvent all of this by concertina-ing them into one decisive, devastatingly effective event called a Project Scoping and Planning session.

The benefits of this approach are:

▶ Projects launched in a day. The project is actually running by the end of the day. There is no quicker and more cost-effective way to begin a project.
▶ Clear project objectives, project requirements and agreement/buy-in on these from the stakeholders.
▶ Accurate estimates upon which firm commitments can be made.
▶ A clear picture of how the project will unfold.
▶ A kick-start to the project.

Scoping and Planning a Project in a Day – How

There are two things that are the key to making this method work for you. The first is to bear in mind that your objective is to end the day with two deliverables – the scope document and the plan. The other thing is that you have to spend the time as wisely as possible on the day to achieve these two deliverables.

So here's how it works:

- ▶ You identify the people who are needed at the 1-day scoping and planning session.
- ▶ There is preparation time before the 1-day session. During this attendees essentially prepare some of the input for the two documents mentioned above. They give this input to you and you consolidate it into first drafts of each document.
- ▶ At the 1-day session, you act as facilitator and you need a second person to act as 'scribe'. Anyone capable of running a project can be a facilitator. The scribe needs to know how to use Word, Excel and MS Project (or their equivalents). During this session, you capture the rest of the input from the attendees and insert it into the documents.
- ▶ There is a completion phase where the two documents are finalised. This generally amounts to little more than prettying them up.

Preparation

Identify all of the people who are entitled to a say in the scope of the project. This needs to include those people who sometimes don't necessarily appear high on the organisation chart, but have the power to change everything at the stroke of a pen.

Find a day when they can all come together. Make it clear to them that the sooner this can be the sooner the project gets on the road. Explain to them that you're intending to scope and plan the project in a day and that this will get their project done quicker. Explain to them also that they will have to do some preparation beforehand, but that the benefit of doing this is that their project should be done quicker.

Between the Preparation and the 1-day session, you are going to end up drafting two documents. These are (a) a scope (goal) of the project and (b) a plan for the project. So send them an email asking them to do some preparation for each of these beforehand. Tell them they should spend no more than half a day on this preparation, and that they should limit themselves to whatever level of detail can be achieved in that time.

For the goal, you want them to do goal setting, exactly as described in Chapter 1. This should take them no more than half an hour.

For the plan, ask them to build a plan for their piece of the project as described in Chapter 2. This should take the rest of their preparation time.

Give them a deadline by when they need to get the stuff back to you. This deadline should be a day or two before the 1-day session to allow you enough time to put together early drafts of the two documents. Using the material that comes back, start putting the two documents together, so that they can be used as a start point on the 1-day session. If no material, or only partial material comes back, don't panic – it can all still work on the day.

The 1-day Session

Welcome everybody. Introduce yourself and explain your role – you're going to run the session and keep everything on schedule. Introduce and explain the role of the scribe. S(he)'s going to record the proceedings so that the plan will be available at the end of the day. Run the day to the following agenda:

09:00–10:45	Using the draft goal document as a start point, do the goal setting for the project as described in Chapter 1.
11:00–13:00	Using the draft plan document as a start point, build the plan as described in Chapter 2. Do as much as you can in the time available.
13:00–13:45	Lunch
13:45–15:00	Build the plan (continued)
15:15–16:15	Do a risk analysis on the plan as described in chapter 4.
16:00–17:00	Reading from the newly-created plan, assign next actions to session attendees. You're done!

HOW YOU NEED TO DO IT
Scoping and Planning a Project in a Day

1. Identify the people you will need.
2. Get them to do their preparation prior to the 1-day session.
3. Consolidate this work into draft versions of the scope and plan documents.
4. Run the 1-day session to the timetable above and complete the two documents.
5. Do a final tidy up of the documents after the 1-day session.

3 Calculate the Value of Getting It Done Early

Since people generally don't believe that projects can be done early they don't bother to look at what the financial impact might be. If they did they might be astonished at what they discovered and, as a result, there could be huge incentive to get the project done early.

The following diagram shows an example of a simple profit model for a project development project. It shows

Profit model for a product development project

All figures in US$ Figures in italics must be entered by the user	Input	Development -Q4	-Q3	-Q2	-Q1	Year 1 Q1	Q2	Q3	Q4	Year 2 Q1	Q2	Q3	Q4
PRODUCT REVENUES													
Average sales price	*350*					350	350	350	350	350	350	350	350
Market size in units						*40,000*	*40,000*	*50,000*	*60,000*	*80,000*	*120,000*	*120,000*	*120,000*
Market share						*20%*	*25%*	*25%*	*25%*	*20%*	*15%*	*15%*	*15%*
Unit sales						8,000	10,000	12,500	15,000	16,000	18,000	18,000	18,000
Dollar sales						2,800,000	3,500,000	4,375,000	5,250,000	5,600,000	6,300,000	6,300,000	6,300,000
PRODUCT COSTS													
Unit cost	*50*					50	50	50	50	50	50	50	50
Cost of goods sold						400,000	500,000	625,000	750,000	800,000	900,000	900,000	900,000
Gross margin in $						2,400,000	3,000,000	3,750,000	4,500,000	4,800,000	5,400,000	5,400,000	5,400,000
Gross margin in %						86%	86%	86%	86%	86%	86%	86%	86%
DEVELOPMENT COSTS													
Cost per team member	*100,000*	100,000	100,000	100,000	100,000	100,000	100,000	100,000	100,000	100,000	100,000	100,000	100,000
Number of team members		2	6	6	4	2	1	0.5	0.5	0.5	0.5	0.5	0.5
Development team cost		200,000	600,000	600,000	400,000	200,000	100,000	50,000	50,000	50,000	50,000	50,000	50,000
Marketing costs	*15%*					420,000	525,000	656,250	787,500	840,000	945,000	945,000	945,000
General & administrative	*5%*					140,000	175,000	218,750	262,500	280,000	315,000	315,000	315,000
Total costs		200,000	600,000	600,000	400,000	760,000	800,000	925,000	1,100,000	1,170,000	1,310,000	1,310,000	1,310,000
PROFIT / LOSS													
Profit (loss) before tax (PBT)		- 200,000	-600,000	- 600,000	- 400,000	2,040,000	2,700,000	3,450,000	4,150,000	4,430,000	4,990,000	4,990,000	4,990,000
Cumulative PBT		- 200,000	-800,000	-1,400,000	-1,800,000	240,000	2,940,000	6,390,000	10,540,000	14,970,000	19,960,000	24,950,000	29,940,000

TOTAL PBT	29,940,000

the cost of developing the product versus the revenues that are projected to be achieved.

Having built such a model it is possible for the project manager and the stakeholders to examine what the effect of finishing early would be. Could they charge a higher price for their product because it's on the market earlier? As a result could they grab a bigger market share? Could being to market early mean that the product's lifetime will be extended?

So, for example, they could see what the effect of:

▶ shortening the project by three months;
▶ charging $400 per unit instead of $350;
▶ assuming a 5% higher market share and an additional quarter's sales but at reduced volume

would be. In this example the profit before tax (PBT) would be $29,940,000 for the unshortened project and $30,240,000 for the shortened project – an additional $300,000.

Equally, they could look at the negative scenario. What if the project runs late? What if it ran over by three months? Then the revenues would be delayed by three months and the costs would continue for a further three months. This would cause the PBT to drop from $29,940,000 to $24,350,000, a loss of over $5.5m! So there would be a big incentive to see that this project wasn't delayed.

4 Lay the Plan Out As a Strip Board

It's already been said that people who run movie projects are good project managers. These people can take a project delivering a product that is part-art, part science and deliver it on time, within budget to a very high degree of quality. And they can do this predictably – over and over again. This being the case then, there is much to be learnt from them about how to run projects properly.

If you ever hear a movie person talking about the shooting of a movie, you'll often hear them say something like, 'It was a 79-day shoot'. Now, when's the last time you heard a project manager say, 'It was a 79-day project'. More often, you're likely to hear them say, 'Where did the week go and what did we achieve?'

Movie people are completely focussed on keeping the number of days shooting their movie as short as possible. There is a very simple reason for this. It's because shooting movies is very expensive. Each day costs a small fortune. So the more the number of days shooting can be kept to a minimum, the cheaper the movie will be to make.

So if you want to learn how to shorten projects or shorten time to market, it's good to know that the problem has already been solved. Movie people have solved it. They know how to run projects in the shortest possible time. Furthermore, the key to it is terribly simple. They merely break everything down to the day level of detail (as opposed to the 1–5 days described in Chapter 2).

When movie people plan the shooting of movie they use what is known as a 'strip board'. Think of a strip board as being like a giant spreadsheet. The rows of the spreadsheet are the days of the shoot. The first series of columns in the spreadsheet list all of the cast members – from the highest paid star to the lowest walk-on part. The remaining columns list all of the other things – props, special effects, animals, special services, equipment and so on – required to shoot on that particular day. Months before a movie is due to be shot, somebody goes through the script [the definition of the goal] and creates a strip board for the movie. The strip board essentially shows what every member of the team is doing every day of the project. Get the idea?

So if you want to get your project done:

> ► in the shortest possible time;
> ► as cheaply as possible;
> ► with the minimum of delays and waste,

plan it down to the day level of detail and document it on a strip board. The following diagram shows an example of a strip board.

Example of a piece of a strip board

Cast (Jobs)

Week	Day	Date	Charlie	Engineer #2	Engineer #3	Marketing people (3)	Admin Assistant
1	1	9-Jan-07	Project kickoff	Project kickoff	Project kickoff	Project kickoff	Project kickoff
	2	10-Jan-07	6 Gather info on competitive products [1/2 day], 8 identify users [1/2 day]				
	3	11-Jan-07	9 Prepare user questionnaires				10 Distribute user questionnaires
	4	12-Jan-07	9 Prepare user questionnaires				11 Retrieve questionnaires
2	5	15-Jan-07	7 Review with Marketing			7 Review with Marketing	
	6	16-Jan-07	12 Analyse information				
	7	17-Jan-07	13 Write requirements document				
	8	18-Jan-07	13 Write requirements document				
	9	19-Jan-07	13 Write requirements document				
3	10	22-Jan-07	13 Write requirements document				
	11	23-Jan-07	13 Write requirements document				
	12	24-Jan-07	13 Write requirements document				
	13	25-Jan-07	13 Write requirements document				
	14	26-Jan-07	13 Write requirements document				
4	15	29-Jan-07	13 Write requirements document				15 Circulate document
	16	30-Jan-07	17,18 Review meeting / changes to document (inc. circulate again)			16, 17 Individual review [1/2 day each] & review meeting [1/2 day]	
	17	31-Jan-07	18 Changes to document				
	18	1-Feb-07	18,19 Changes to document (inc. circulate again)				
	19	2-Feb-07	20-22 Second review / Signoff / Reqs complete [1/4 day]			20-22 Second review / Signoff / Reqs complete [1/4 day]	20-22 Second review / Signoff / Reqs complete [1/4 day]
5	20	5-Feb-07	58 Prototype	58 Prototype	58 Prototype		

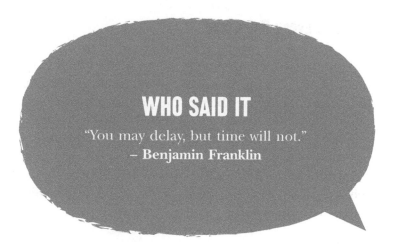

WHO SAID IT

"You may delay, but time will not."
– Benjamin Franklin

5 Do a Mission Briefing for the Team and for the Stakeholders

The idea of a 'mission briefing' is taken from those old black and white movies about WW II bombing missions where the bomber crews are taken through the plan by their management. What a mission briefing means in this context is to take the team through the project plan line by line, asking them to look for opportunities to shorten the project. It is almost inevitable that they will come up with some.

Exactly the same but this time the audience is the stakeholder. While they may be less likely to find opportunities for shortening the project, a mission briefing can be a good way of showing them why what they're asking you to do is impossible.

6 Make Every Day Count

In Fred Brooks, *The Mythical Man-Month* (see Chapter 1) the author poses the question, 'how did the project get to be late?', the answer being, 'the project got to be late one day at a time'. Well, the project also gets to be early one day at a time. If you think in terms of spending each day wisely – making every day count – you will find that opportunities to shorten the project will present themselves as the project unfolds. Here are eight specific things that you can do:

1. Don't do it tomorrow if it can be done today. Encourage an attitude of 'can I finish this today'?
2. Encourage everybody to be hypersensitive to changes that increase the scope of the project.
3. If team members find themselves waiting for somebody else, get them to raise an alert.
4. If team members are aware of a potential delay coming up, flag it as soon as it's known.
5. Keep Dance Cards up to date. This way people will know if they've over allocated themselves. Better still is to use the Dance Card to avoid over allocating themselves in the first place.
6. If team members can start a job early, do so.
7. If they can finish a job early without compromising quality, do so.
8. If a piece of the project can be delivered using a simpler or quicker approach, then do so.

7 O'Connell's Law

It's not a particularly common phenomenon but when it happens it's glorious. For want of a better name I have called it O'Connell's Law. It says that once a team finds itself ahead of schedule it will try to get even more ahead of schedule. So, if you can once get ahead of schedule, you get a snowball effect. The team want to pull ahead even further. If you can once get some traction, using any of the techniques described above, you will find that the chances of your project coming in early increase enormously.

WHAT YOU NEED TO READ

▶ 'How to Defend an Unpopular Schedule' is an article by Steve McConnell, which can be found at *www.stevemcconnell.com/art.htm*. Steve is the author of numerous books on software project management. The article may be about software schedules but the lessons are universal.

▶ *www.helium.com* – contains some useful articles on managing stakeholder expectations. Go to *www.helium.com* and do a search on 'managing stakeholder expectations.'

▶ *Getting to Yes: Negotiating an Agreement Without Giving In* by Roger Fisher and William Ury (Random House, 2003) is a great book on negotiation. If you like the idea of negotiating using the facts, as described in this chapter, this book will give you further ideas to develop your negotiating ability.

▶ *Critical Chain Project Management* by Lawrence P. Leach (Artech House, 2004) is not light reading but if you're interested in shortening projects, shortening time to market, getting projects done in the shortest possible time, this book, based on the work of the brilliant Eli Goldratt, is a must.

▶ *How to Run Successful Projects in Web Time* (Artech House, 2000) is another one of my books, and despite the title, this has nothing to do with web projects. Rather it too is about shortening projects using ideas taken from the movie-making industry.

▶ *Developing Products in Half the Time* by Preston G. Smith and Donald G. Reinertsen (John Wiley & Sons Ltd, 1997) is another excellent book if you're trying to get projects done more quickly.

IF YOU ONLY REMEMBER ONE THING

Don't ever say yes to an impossible mission. If you do you will be condemned to a miserable project. And sooner or later it will all end in tears.

CHAPTER 6

TRACKING AND STATUS REPORTING

WHAT IT'S ALL ABOUT

USING THE PLAN AS INSTRUMENTATION TO DRIVE THE PROJECT

If you think about it, what you do in Chapters 1–5 is that you (a) build a realistic plan and then (b) tell the stakeholders what's possible and what's not possible. As a result you get agreement with them about how the project will proceed.

Once the project begins, you have to do the mirror image of these two things, because now what you have to do is (a) update the plan and (b) once again tell the stakeholders what's happening. So you see, the focus is always on the stakeholders – as it should be if your objective is 'happy stakeholders'.

WHO SAID IT

"Reality is that which, when you stop believing in it, doesn't go away."
– Philip K. Dick

It was said earlier that the plan is a model of the project. In other words, it tells you what should be happening on the project. Then you want to ensure that what happens on the project gets reflected in the plan, so that the two things stay in sync over the life of the project. Another way to think about this is that the plan is the instrumentation you will use to drive the project.

MANAGING PEOPLE

In the course of your project you will have to manage people. While this is not a book on how to do that, it should offer some guidance that will help you in this most difficult of tasks. So this is what the next couple of sections are about. There is also a separate section on dealing with problem people/situations.

It's true to say that each of us, depending on our personality, has what could be called our 'natural' management style. Some people are very hands off. 'There's no point in having a dog,' the saying goes, 'and barking yourself'. In other words, if somebody has a job to do leave them to get on with it and trust that they will do it properly. Then, on the other end of the spectrum, there are people who are very hands-on. Only by micromanaging everything do they feel that they're in control and can they be sure that things are on track. Which is right? The former sounds like a nice regime to work under – the person being managed can use their own initiative and creativity

– but it sounds like things could go a long way wrong here before they were spotted. The latter regime sounds a lot more safe and secure, but it also sounds like it could be a giant pain to work under (or indeed to have to apply) such a regime.

The answer, of course, is that one size doesn't fit everybody and that no matter what your personality causes you to do 'naturally', you're going to have to be a bit more versatile when it comes to managing people. The rest of this section offers some guidance on that. It shows you when hands-on is good and when hands-on can be a disaster. Equally, it shows you why hands-off is not always a good idea.

When you assign a job to a person, what follows is a very simple way you could categorise the assignments. It comes from Chapter 3 from the section 'Harnessing the strengths of the team'. Obviously this scheme is somewhat arbitrary, but it will give you a framework within which to locate situations that you encounter yourself. Remember that the scheme was:

1. **Superstar**
2. **Good Citizen**
3. **Don't Report To Me**
4. **New To The Job**
5. **No Availability**
6. **Can't Do The Job**

Now here's how to deal with these situations – *irrespective of what your personality would cause you to do.*

USING DIFFERENT MANAGEMENT STYLES

1. **Superstar.** Just let them get on with it. Micromanaging this person is (a) just going to upset/annoy them and (b) is a complete waste of your time. Leave them alone and they'll come back to you when the thing is done. This is not to say to ignore them completely but any interaction with these people is likely to be along the lines of 'what are you doing for the weekend?' or 'did you see the match last night?' It is very safe to delegate to these people.

2. **Good Citizen.** With these guys you're not going to be quite so blasé. You want to keep an eye on them but not so much that it turns into micro-management. So here's how that might work. Say they're working on a three day job – Monday, Tuesday, Wednesday. You might go along at the end of Monday to check on things. What you'd like to see is (a) some progress – maybe five of the twenty widgets have been processed or the first section of the document has been written – something like that - and (b) that they have a little plan of how they're going to get to the end. They're saying, 'I hope to be this far by the end of Tuesday and then I'll finish it off on Wednesday morning with Wednesday afternoon for contingency'. If they had made some progress and had such a plan, you could perhaps lighten off a

little bit. Equally, if they hadn't and didn't, you might suggest a little plan to them and say that you'd check with them again about Tuesday lunchtime. (So you can see you can be very sensitive with this method, applying a little push where it's needed, leaving it alone where it isn't.)

3. **Don't Report To Me.** It may sound that there's not a lot you can do here. In reality, there's lots. It starts out when you estimate the job in the first place. Get the person involved to give you the estimate. If they're known to be an incredibly busy or under-pressure sort of person (or maybe even if they're not), query the estimate with them. Are they sure that they'll be able to do this? Can you depend on this commitment? Show them your plan and show them what the negative effect will be if they fail to deliver what they're promising. Then, as the time approaches when they must do this thing for you, send them a reminder or remind them if you meet them in the cafeteria or the corridor. Then, perhaps the day before the thing is due to start, an email. Are we good to go? Anything they need? Any excuse to nudge them again. (You may be saying to yourself that you shouldn't have to baby sit people in this way but unfortunately, in project management, sometimes you have to in order to get the job done.) Will all of this guarantee that they come through for you? Of course not. So if it all goes horribly wrong go back to them and reschedule the

thing. Also make it clear to them how badly this has affected you. If it's serious enough you may have to put it in the status report (see below). And then, only if the person fails to deliver again, do you escalate it in some way – to their boss, to your boss etc. So you see, rather than being powerless in these situations, there's plenty you can do.

4. **New To The Job.** This is the situation that calls for micromanagement. A hands-off approach here will just cause problems. Not only that, hands-off would mean that you were guilty of throwing the person in the deep end to see if they sank or floated. Not a good idea. So here we're talking handholding, nurturing, training courses, on the job training, shadowing them, keeping a close eye on them, correcting them when they go wrong, passing on the benefit for your knowledge – in the hope that, as quickly as possible, they become useful members of society and you don't have to do that any more. (But notice that if they don't – and their 'report card' would show this – then you're just going to have to keep on them.)

5. **No Availability.** Here you have a job (demand) for which you thought you had supply. Now it turns out you don't. Now, you'll have to find it somewhere else. You'll have to do this job yourself or somebody else will have to do it or somebody will have to suck it up. This will involve you in lots of management effort (i.e. definitely

not hands-off) until you sort out this problem. And if that person has a number of jobs to do on your project, and they've got an availability problem with all of them, then that leaves you with an even bigger supply / demand imbalance that you have to solve. Lots of hands-on here.

6. **Can't Do The Job.** Here you have two problems. The first is as in the previous paragraph – how will you get this job done? How will you find supply to match the demand? But now you have the other problem of what are you going to do about this person? You've got a problem person or situation. Read on.

DEALING WITH PROBLEM PEOPLE/SITUATIONS

Specifically, these situations are where you give somebody a job to do and – repeatedly – they screw it up. What are you to do in these circumstances?

What follows is a four step process that you could go through in these situations.

Step 1

The first thing to ask yourself is whether it is you – and not they – who is the problem. Did you make clear what you wanted? Were you available to answer questions or to clarify things? Did you give them the resources – people, equipment, materials, training, support or whatever - to get the job done? Did *you* give *them* an impossible mission? Because if you're guilty of any of these things, then it shouldn't really come as any great surprise if they failed. Try to be honest here. It's all too easy to see the other person as the problem. But maybe the problem actually starts with you. If, having done this, you find that you were at fault, then correct whatever you did and see what happens. Maybe the problem goes away.

Step 2

If however, the problem fails to go away or you weren't at fault in the first place, then you need to move to this which is where you come up with an improvement plan. An improvement plan is simply a list of actions that you, the company or the person is going to take, along with dates by which those things are going to happen. (And just to be clear, you're not talking long deadlines here – you're looking at a handful of weeks.) While you or the company may do one or two things – 'organise training' or 'monitor more closely' – things like that - the bulk of the actions will be undertaken by the person. In other words, the onus is on them to do the improving. This may solve the problem. If not, you go to step 3.

Step 3

Step 3 involves what you can think of as an extreme improvement plan – again with short deadlines. Basically, step 3 is an ultimatum and is pretty much all about the person – take these actions, improve these things or something very bad will happen. This may solve the problem. If not then go to step 4.

Step 4

This is where the very bad thing happens. It can range from moving them off the project team to firing. What you actually choose will probably end up being a function of (a) the type of organisation you are (public sector versus private sector, for example) and (b) the culture of the organisation. Also, it will almost certainly involve the Human Resources department –as indeed, will step 3. Needless to say, all of the actions at each of the steps should be documented.

THE PROJECT MANAGER'S DAILY ROUTINE

The Project Manager's Daily Routine is a 'light' way to track the project and update the plan. In one neat package it does a number of things which are very important as you execute the project. These are:

▶ It provides a status check on the project.

▶ It enables you to drive the project forward.

▶ It gives you a structure within which to deal with fire fights on the project.

▶ It enables you to record what actually happens on the project, compare this against your estimates and use all of this to improve your estimating.

▶ It enables you to do change control i.e. to make the right choice when changes occur on your project.

And finally, do you have to do it every day? Well, we'll answer that question as well.

Project Meetings

Most project meetings may be seen to be a complete waste of time. They turn into talking shops where people who like the sound of their own voices can sound important. Or they end up as long rambling discussions about technical issues on the project – of little or no interest to many of the people at the meeting. Or the project team spend their time trying to gives excuses as to why they haven't made more progress. Or they try to imply progress that hasn't actually been made.

HOW YOU NEED TO DO IT

The Project Manager's Daily Routine

1. Look down the plan from top to bottom and identify any task that requires some action by you today.
2. These are your to-do's on this project for today.
3. Do these actions.
4. For each task completed record the results (actual work, actual start and end, actual duration) in the plan. These can be just extra columns in your Gantt Chart. Any task on your project should only be regarded as being in one of two states – either done or not done. There should be no use of percentage complete or things like '90% done' or 'we're nearly there'. (Because the tasks have been broken down to the low level of detail previously described this should not cause anyone a problem. However, a – supposedly – small task that remains not done for a long time, should set alarm bells off. The task is clearly not as small as everybody thought it was.)
5. For each incident (unexpected event) that occurs on the project, determine whether or not it's a big change. All of the following should be regarded as big changes:

    a. Changes to the scope (demand) of the project e.g. 'we don't want a glass, we want a swimming pool.'

    b. Changes to the resourcing (supply) e.g. 'you can't have your two test engineers.'

    c. Assumptions turning out not to be true e.g. we assumed we would have to process fifty widgets but it now turns out to be hundred.

    d. For big changes, revise the plan based on the new conditions and present this to the stakeholders exactly as described in Chapter 5. The stakeholders then have a choice. They can accept the new plan – with its new deadline, resourcing, costs and all the rest of it. In this case, this new plan becomes the one you now work from. Alternatively, they can say that they don't want to go with the new plan. This must mean then that the decisions about scope, resourcing or assumptions will have to be reversed and the original plan reverted to.

6. For each incident which isn't a big change either use contingency to cover it or work more.

7. Check to see whether the date and budget have changed. If they haven't then the project is

on target. If they have improved, say nothing. If they have dis-improved then this is a warning sign. A single dis-improvement by itself may not be a problem, since the slip could be corrected before the next time you run the Daily Routine. But if, on several successive runnings of the Daily Routine, the trend is not in the right direction, then this is a sign that you're in trouble. One way or the other, you need to communicate the resulting status to the stakeholders.

How often should you hold project meetings? In most cases, weekly is the best. There may be occasions where you might want to have them more often than that. Say, for example, there was a critical project which had to go live on a certain day and was in its last couple of weeks, you might want to have daily meetings to ensure that there were no slip-ups in reaching the target. Do what seems sensible. If the meetings start to seem to be a bit pointless maybe reduce the regularity. On the other hand, if lots of slip-ups are happening then maybe you need more regular meetings.

If you're going to have a project meeting, then it's important that everybody knows what the purpose of the meeting is. Typically, the meeting has three purposes:

1. To gather progress from the team so that the status report can be prepared.
2. To deal with any issues on the project.
3. To ensure that everybody knows what has to be done next.

Allocate times for each of these and you've got your agenda. Remember that a list of things to do is not an agenda. An agenda is a list of things to do along with the times allocated to each of these items. There's an example in 'Scoping and Planning a Project in a Day' in Chapter 5.

To gather progress from the team, go round each person in turn and find out whether the jobs they had to do in the period you're looking at have been completed. As discussed earlier, there is no third possibility. This should reduce significantly the likelihood of people rambling on about their work.

Go round a second time, find out if there are any issues which are holding things up or causing obstacles and deal with them. In addition, ask everybody to calculate a PSI for the project. Use any low scores to probe for further issues or problems.

Go round a third time and ask each person to say what they're planning to do in the upcoming period. Get them to confirm that they have everything they need and that they're have taken account of any dependencies on other members of the team.

Finally, ask if there is any other business, deal with it if there is, and you're out. There's an argument that you don't actually need project meetings at all. If you have worked your plan out to the level of detail described, if you're tracking it properly as just explained and if each task can only exist on one of two states (done or not done), then why have a meeting? You as the project manager can go round and find out what tasks people have completed and that's all you need. Notice too the value of doing this. You don't tie people up at a meeting that maybe isn't that relevant to them. They spend the bulk of their time working on their tasks to get the project done. Which is exactly what they should be doing.

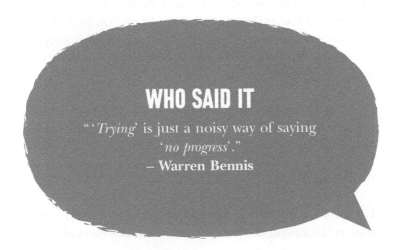

WHO SAID IT

"'*Trying*' is just a noisy way of saying '*no progress*'."
– Warren Bennis

Status Reporting

Once you have determined the status of the project you then need to communicate that to the stakeholders. You have 100% knowledge about what is going on on the project, but is that what you communicate to the stakeholders?

Absolutely not! There is stuff going on on the project that you would probably never want the stakeholders to know. This then raises the idea that you are going to filter the information to the stakeholders. Specifically, what is meant by this is the following:

> ► If things are going well – and you will know this from your tracking – you need to tell the stakeholders that. But you don't want to say it in a hysterical, we-could-be-coming-in-three-months-early kind of way. Instead you just want to say, 'We're okay. We'll get back to you if there's a problem.'
>
> ► Equally, if things are going badly, you want to tell the stakeholders that. But you don't want to spring it on them; you don't want them going along happily and suddenly open up a trapdoor underneath them. Instead, if things have begun to take a turn for the worst, you can start to get the stakeholders ready for that. As a result, if you then end up having to tell them that the schedule is going to slip or the budget is going to be blown, they're prepared for it and maybe

have begun to make their own plans. Thus, it is possible to imagine a project that maybe went very wrong from the point of view of the dates and budgets and where one could still end up with happy stakeholders – provided you handled the stakeholders gently as just described. Your objective then, will be to do exactly this.

There's one other thing about status reporting that's worth saying. There's a Dilbert cartoon – you may have seen it. In it, Dilbert and his colleagues are having a meeting. The boss says, 'Let's go round the table and give an update on each of our projects.' Dilbert says, 'My project is a pathetic series of poorly-planned, near-random acts. My life is a tragedy of emotional desperation.' The boss says that 'It's more or less customary to say that things are going fine.' Dilbert says, 'I think I need a hug.'

What the boss says is so true – it *is* more or less customary to say that things are going fine. And this is what most of the status reporting that you see and hear does. Let's look at some of them – the verbal ones first.

You ask how's it going and you're told it's 'fine' or 'great' or 'everything's on target' or 'everything's under control' or the terrifying 'we're 90% done' – which generally means that ninety percent of the time has gone, not that 90% of the thing has been done.

And then you get the written status reports that are full of things like 'tasks completed last week', 'tasks planned for next week', 'percentage complete', 'critical issues' and so on – lots of data, not a lot of information. So, if you're to do status reporting it had better be useful and it had better be honest. The next section tells you how.

HOW YOU NEED TO DO IT – STATUS REPORTING

You need to do status reporting in three levels. Level 1 is a small amount of critical information. Level 2 adds extra detail and finally, level 3 gives everything and the kitchen sink. Here they are in turn:

Level 1

Are we on target or not? Are we going to hit the date or not? If the only thing you're tracking is the date, then that's all you need. If you're also tracking the budget and/or the work (person-days) then you would also say whether they are on target or not.

You could use what is known as RAG or traffic light reporting. Green means you have a plan and you're running to the plan. Amber means you've drifted a bit but you're taking steps to bring things back on track. Red means the plan is gone to hell and the project will have to be replanned.

The only other thing that you might want to put in Level 1 is what you can think of as 'I need help'. This is where there might be an issue that is outside your control or authority to resolve. Maybe you need help from your boss or other stakeholders to get resources. Or maybe there is some roadblock in the project that you want help in removing because you're unable to do it. Or maybe you need a decision made – you don't care what it is, you just want it made, maybe by the stakeholders.

If this was the case, then you would also put into Level 1:

- ▶ What – here's the issue.
- ▶ Action – here's what I want done about it.
- ▶ Who – here's who has to do this.
- ▶ Deadline – here's when it has to be done by.
- ▶ Threat – here's what will happen if it isn't done.

So, for example, you might say, 'I need two test engineers by July 31st. My boss is the person who has to get these. For every day they're late after July 31st, the project will be a day late'. (Nothing like a threat to focus the mind!)

Level 2

What tends to be missing from many status reports is a history of how the project got to be where it now is. If you don't provide a history, stakeholders will provide their own. In general, if this happens, their history will not be favourable to you. So, for instance, supposing a project was meant to finish on September 21st of a particular year and it now looks like finishing on November

29th, what will the stakeholders think or say? Almost certainly, they'll start to talk in terms of 'the slip'.

So, in order to avoid this scenario, you need to interpret the dates for them. You (and nobody else) needs to write the history and explain how the project got to be where it is. Here's how to do that. (It's described for the date. If you're tracking the budget and/or the work, then you would do it for those as well.) For the date, you would say:

▶ Here's what it was originally.
▶ Here's what it is now.
▶ Here's how it changed. (You would have a line for each time the date changed along with an explanation of when and why it changed.)

Level 3

Finally, in Level 3, you could give any remaining information that you think would be useful. This might include:

▶ The plan (on a Gantt Chart, for example).
▶ The latest Risk Analysis.
▶ By all means list 'tasks completed last week'. This is good for team morale and showing progress to stakeholders.
▶ 'Tasks planned for next week' is also good. It reminds the team that, however this week may have gone, they're going to have to do it all again next week.

WHO YOU NEED TO KNOW
Frederick Morgan

Lieutenant General Frederick Morgan was the man responsible for planning Operation Overlord, the invasion of Nazi-occupied north-western Europe in WWII. The ultimate goal of this project was the destruction of German forces and the defeat of Germany. Morgan had to work backwards from that result to determine what manpower and material were required to complete the task. There had never been an amphibious invasion of this size and Morgan and his staff had to plan the detail of the operation. In 1943 and 1944, while doing this planning, Morgan worked in a room over a shop in the West End of London. With a military assistant he often went into a Marylebone hotel, where he started debates among the customers about sending an attack across the Channel. He wanted to know what the ordinary civilian was thinking. He said, 'Sound opinion is not the exclusive prerogative of those who are paid to give it.'

Send out your status report once a week – probably towards close of business on that week. This chapter talked earlier about RAG reporting but there's also SAS reporting. It stands for Send and Scarper. So you've got the picture – your status report is there on your screen, your bag is packed, you've got your hat and coat on, the engine of your car is running, then you hit 'Send', run out the door before anybody has had a chance to read it and switch your mobile phone or Blackberry off!

Because – if you've planned it properly, tracked it properly and reported it honestly, the stakeholders can't really ask for more than that. You're entitled to a life – and we'll be saying lots more about that in Chapter 8.

WHO SAID IT

"Human beings, who are almost unique in having the ability to learn from the experience of others, are also remarkable for their apparent disinclination to do so."
– **Douglas Adams**

PROJECT POST-MORTEMS

It's a terrible name and almost any name would be better. There are lots – 'post-project reviews', 'post-implementation reviews', the military call them 'after-action reviews', in telecommunications company Ericsson they're known as 'opportunities for improvement', others call them 'lessons learnt', 'do differentlies'. The key thing is to learn something from a completed project so that you can carry this learning over to your next one.

It has to be said that post-mortems aren't done anywhere near as much as they should be. If the project was a failure, everybody just wants to forget about it. If it's a success, it's almost like everybody is so surprised they want to move on eagerly to the next big thing and the post-mortem gets lost along the way.

Sometimes, even when they are done, post-mortems suffer the same fate as those government reports that get produced from time to time and have lots of recommendations in them. The report ends up on the shelf, the recommendations are never carried out and you might as well not have done the post-mortem in the first place. So two sections follow. The first one describes how to do a post-mortem. The second one describes a 'light' post-mortem that (a) would have a good chance of being done, (b) could be done very quickly and (c) would have a good chance of having its recommendations implemented.

HOW YOU NEED TO DO IT
A Project Post-Mortem

1. Tell everybody who was involved in the project – team, customer, management and any other stakeholders – that you are doing a post-mortem to round out the project. Ask them for a contribution. Tell them you want them to be blunt, and that all the submissions will be gathered together into a final document which will be published. Those inside the company will get the whole document; those outside will get a version which has had any stuff confidential to your company removed. (The latter allows you to involve the customer, subcontractors or any other outside organisations, but still be the final arbiter of what goes to them.) Participation is optional and anonymity is allowed.
2. Give them some simple guidelines:
3. You're expecting 1–3 pages.
4. Essentially you want them to write a 'how was it for you?' essay. You want them to give their story of the project.

5. They should give both positives and negatives; what was done well, what was done badly.

6. You're particularly interested in any rules of thumb or other estimating type data that may be of value to other members of the team.

7. Ask them to list the number one or top two or three key lessons they would take away from the project.

8. Give them a closing date for submissions.

9. In the meantime you write an objective account of the project. Write it like a police report. Confine yourself to the facts and keep your own opinions out of it. If you like, you can also write a 'how was it for you?' essay, but make clear which is which, and the difference between the two. Make sure you capture estimated versus actual data i.e. here's what you estimated, here's what actually happened, so that you can see where your estimating needs to be improved next time out.

10. When all your material is in, gather it together, generate the version for outside the organisation and publish both versions (the internal and external ones).

11. You might also like to put the estimating data into some central repository where everyone can access it. If this is the first time this has ever been done, make a big song and dance about it – your organisation's historical project database has just been born.

12. Ensure that somebody does something as a result of the post-mortem e.g. an improvement project is put in place, or a single improvement is made or the top three suggestions are acted on or something. Don't just let the audit gather dust.

THE DIRTY DOZEN – THE TWELVE MOST COMMON REASONS WHY PROJECTS FAIL

During your project management life you may come across projects that have gotten into trouble. If your job is to figure out what went wrong, then check the following dirty dozen first. There's a good chance that you'll find your answer here.

1. The goal of the project isn't defined properly.

2. The goal of the project is defined properly, but then changes to it aren't controlled.

201

HOW YOU NEED TO DO IT
A Light Post-Mortem

If you think that a full post-mortem as just described is unlikely to be done on your project, then make sure that you at least do a light one. Here's how to do that: You're going to do three things. They are:

▶ Record the actual versus estimated. (If you did the tracking as described above, then you will have the plan with the actuals in your hand on the day the project ends. In other words, no extra effort is required to get you this.

▶ Write down the number one (or maybe top two or three) thing that was done well on the project – some little technique you developed, or template you came up with or piece of knowledge you uncovered that really made a difference. Usually, post-mortems tend to focus on things that were done badly, but it's also worth exploring what was done well. Often we fail to realise the significance of certain things and so we fail to carry those things over. So be sure to check it out.

And once you have identified something share it with your colleagues. In this way you, but also the organisation, may get some step improvements in the way projects are carried out.

▶ And then, of course, what was done badly? Again maybe the number one or top two or three. What were the things which, had we known them, we would have done differently? Again, share it with our colleagues. It's a bit harder to do this – nobody likes to admit to mistakes – but again, it might result in some improvement across the organisation.

3. Not all of the project stakeholders are identified.
4. Stakeholders are identified but win conditions aren't.
5. The project isn't planned/estimated properly.
6. The project isn't led properly.
7. The project is planned/estimated properly but then it isn't resourced as was planned.
8. The project is planned such that it has no contingency.
9. The expectations of project participants aren't managed.

10. The project is planned properly but then progress against the plan is not monitored and controlled properly.

11. Project reporting is inadequate or non-existent.

12. When projects get in to trouble, people believe the problem can be solved by some simple action, e.g. work harder, extend the deadline, add more resources. When projects get into trouble, the project needs to be re-planned.

RESCUING PROJECTS THAT HAVE GOTTEN INTO TROUBLE

It may be that you get called upon to do a project rescue. If you do then this is what you need to know.

A rescue is needed when a project goes off the rails. The project was meant to go from A to B. It actually went from A to C. The first thing is to figure out what went wrong. Check out the dirty dozen first. It's almost certain your answer lies there. Also do a PSI on the project as described in Chapter 4. This will point out to you the things that need to be fixed.

Given that the project is now at B you need to do a plan which (a) fixes the things that need to be fixed and (b) puts the project back on target to get to C. You know how to build a plan – it's what's in the first four chapters of this book. So now you do this. Then you sell your new plan to the stakeholders as described in Chapter 5 and hey, you're up and running again.

WHAT YOU NEED TO READ

▶ 4PM, a professional firm of practicing project managers, has a good article on tracking and reporting status on their website (*www.4pm.com/articles*). Project Perfect (*www.projectperfect.com.au*) also has useful information on the subject.

▶ Register at *gantthead.com* to get access to lots of project management things including a good template for doing a project post-mortem.

▶ If you want to get serious about tracking large projects and their projects, then *Project Management Accounting: Budgeting, Tracking and Reporting Costs and Profitability* by Kevin R. Callahan, Gary R. Stetz and Lynn M. Brooks (John Wiley & Sons Ltd, 2007) is a good book.

▶ If you need to know about the Earned Value method of project tracking, then *Earned Value Project Management* by Quentin W. Fleming and Joel M. Koppelman (PMI, 2006) is your bible.

▶ *The One-page Project Manager: Communicate and Manage Any Project with a Single Sheet of Paper* by Clark A. Campbell (John Wiley & Sons Ltd, 2006) is also good on status reporting.

IF YOU ONLY REMEMBER ONE THING

A week is also a long time in a project. So at the very worst, track your project and report its status once a week.

CHAPTER 7

RUNNING MULTIPLE PROJECTS

WHAT IT'S ALL ABOUT

- ▶ The Immutable Laws of Project Management
- ▶ Prioritising
- ▶ Defining Multiple Projects
- ▶ The issues when running multiple projects
- ▶ Careers in project management
- ▶ What makes a good project manager

THE IMMUTABLE LAWS OF PROJECT MANAGEMENT

Now that you know how to run a project it's time to introduce you to the Immutable Laws of Project Management. This is something that has been around for a while now but much of it is chillingly true. While its authorship appears to be lost in the mists of time, it really should be compulsory reading for anybody involved in project management. Additional comments are in square brackets.

▶ **LAW 1:** No major project is ever completed on time, within budget, with the same staff that started it, nor does the project do what it is supposed to do. It is highly unlikely that yours will be the first [unless you do as we described in the preceding six chapters].

Corollary 1: The benefits will be smaller than initially estimated, if estimates were made at all.

Corollary 2: The system finally installed will be completed late and will not do what it is supposed to do.

Corollary 3: It will cost more but will be technically successful.

▶ **LAW 2:** One advantage of fuzzy project objectives is that they let you avoid embarrassment in estimating the corresponding costs. [Apart from that there are nothing but disadvantages.]

▶ **LAW 3:** The effort required to correct a project that is off course increases geometrically with time.

Corollary 1: The longer you wait, the harder it gets.

Corollary 2: If you wait until the project is completed, it's too late.

Corollary 3: Do it now regardless of the embarrassment.

▶ **LAW 4:** The project purpose statement you wrote and understand will be seen differently by everyone else. [So make sure you get the stakeholders to sign it off.]

Corollary 1: If you explain the purpose so clearly that no one could possibly misunderstand, someone will.

Corollary 2: If you do something that you are sure will meet everyone's approval, someone will not like it.

▶ **LAW 5:** Measurable benefits are real. Intangible benefits are not measurable, thus intangible benefits are not real.

Corollary 1: Intangible benefits are real if you can prove that they are real.

▶ **LAW 6:** Anyone who can work effectively on a project part-time certainly does not have enough to do now. [Availability is the silent killer of projects.]

Corollary 1: If a boss will not give a worker a full-time job, you shouldn't either.

Corollary 2: If the project participant has a time conflict, the work given by the full-time boss will not suffer.

▶ **LAW 7:** The greater the project's technical complexity, the less you need a technician to manage it. [Incredibly technical projects can be run by incredibly non-technical people. This is because the currency a project manager deals in is jobs and whether they are complete are not. The techies will figure out the jobs and make the estimates but they will almost certainly need help, guidance and training to do it properly.]

Corollary 1: Get the best manager you can. The manager will get the technicians.

Corollary 2: The reverse of corollary 1 is almost never true.

Corollary 3: In general, great technicians make lousy estimators.

▶ **LAW 8:** A carelessly planned project will take three times longer to complete than expected. A carefully planned project will only take twice as long. [A little planning is better than a lot of fire fighting.]

Corollary 1: If nothing can possibly go wrong, it will anyway.

▶ **LAW 9:** When the project is going well, something will go wrong.

Corollary 1: When things cannot get any worse, they will.

Corollary 2: When things appear to be going better, you have overlooked something.

▶ **LAW 10:** Project teams detest weekly progress reporting because it so vividly manifests their lack of progress [see previous chapter on Project Status Meetings].

▶ **LAW 11:** Projects progress rapidly until they are 90% complete. Then they remain 90% complete forever.

▶ **LAW 12:** If project content is allowed to change freely, the rate of change will exceed the rate of progress.

▶ **LAW 13:** If the user does not believe in the system, a parallel system will be developed. Neither system will work very well.

▶ **LAW 14:** Benefits achieved are a function of the thoroughness of the post-audit check.

Corollary 1: The prospect of an independent post-audit check provides the project team with a powerful incentive to deliver a good system on schedule within budget.

▶ **LAW 15:** No law is immutable. [While many of these things might not, in the strict sense of the word, be described as laws, they are things which occur over and over again on projects. Make sure they don't happen on yours.]

WHO SAID IT

"Project management is like juggling three balls – time, cost and quality. Programme management is like a troupe of circus performers standing in a circle, each juggling-three balls and swapping balls from time to time."
– Geoff Reiss

PRIORITISING

In this and the next chapter you'll need to know about prioritising, so let's define it here. There's some confusion about the term.

Prioritising is *not* saying that you have five priority one things to do, nineteen priority two things and forty-seven priority three things. Prioritising is looking at a list of things and saying, 'if I could only do one thing what would it be?' That then becomes your number one priority. Then you repeat the question with the remaining list to give your number two priority, your number three priority and so on. You can't have a joint priority – like a 7(a) and a 7(b). Each item is either less important or more important than each other item.

DEFINING MULTIPLE PROJECTS

In any discussion of multiple projects it won't be long before you hear reference to the terms, 'project portfolio management', 'programme management', 'project office' and 'programme office'. What are these things and how do they relate to what's already been talked about?

▶ While there are different (and fancier) definitions of project portfolio management and programme management, it is perfectly acceptable to think of 'programmes' and 'portfolios of projects' as both being collections of projects.

▶ It is equally acceptable to think of programmes and portfolios of projects as being nothing more than large projects.

▶ Another definition that is useful when thinking about the difference between programme and project management is that 'programme management is doing the right projects; project management is doing the projects right'.

▶ Project and programme offices are departments or groups set up to support projects and programmes. They can provide some or all of the following: documentation, standards, guidance, support, metrics and policing.

The issue with programmes, portfolios of projects and multiple projects tends not to be what they are called, but rather how they are run. Here's the way many organisations run. Maybe it sounds familiar?

THE ISSUES WHEN RUNNING MULTIPLE PROJECTS

A new year comes round and the organisation has ambitious plans for the year. Grow this by 15%. Reduce that by something else. In addition there are a bunch of new things they want to try and do – products, services, initiatives. And so a bunch of projects (programmes, portfolios of projects) are launched to achieve all of these things. Many people already have a day job to do and they are given a project load on top of this.

The year kicks off and almost immediately, some project starts to fall behind schedule. People begin to work longer hours to get it back on track. Maybe this works, maybe it doesn't. But whether it does or not, it isn't long before some other project starts to drift. Depending on its importance or who jumps up and down the most, resources (people) are shifted onto this project. That brings this one back on track but – inevitably – it causes slippage some place else. The year continues like this with:

▶ everybody working harder and harder;
▶ constant switching of people between projects;
▶ major stress due to all of this.

Finally, the end of the year comes round. Some projects get done and some don't. But it wasn't really the management that decided which projects would be done and which wouldn't. Rather it just depended on what projects got into trouble, how people got shunted around and who managed to put in the biggest effort and do the most sucking it up. Fate/luck running your projects? You said it.

It's possible to get away from all this. Using the ideas discussed already, notably:

- ▶ supply and demand;
- ▶ planning before doing,

it is possible to run the organisation's projects such that:

- ▶ the management takes back the right of deciding which projects get done;
- ▶ the projects are carried out successfully.

How to do that is described in the next section.

WHO SAID IT

"Perhaps when a man has special knowledge and special powers like my own, it rather encourages him to seek a complex explanation when a simpler one is at hand."
– **Sherlock Holmes**

HOW YOU NEED TO DO IT
Starting Out

1. Set the period of time you want to look at
   – three months, six months, a year, whatever.
   The first time you do this, a year is probably
   best.
2. Make a list of all the projects that have to be
   done.
3. For each of these projects work out (by
   estimating as described in Chapter 2) how much
   work (nor duration) is involved in each of these
   projects.
4. Add up all of these individual amounts of work
   to give the total amount of project work that the
   organisation is trying to accomplish in the given
   period. This is the demand.
5. Now figure out how many people are available
   to work on projects over the same period. Make
   a list of these people.
6. Figure out how much time each of them can
   devote to the projects over the same period,
   taking their day jobs or other commitments into
   account. (Use Dance Cards, if necessary, to do
   this.)

7. Add up all of these amounts work. This is the supply.
8. If the supply is less than or equal to the demand, then you're in business.
9. However, this is rarely the case. In reality, demand usually exceeds supply. If this is the case then you need to prioritise the projects as described earlier. Ask the question, 'If I could only do one project, what would it be?' That project then becomes your number one priority. Now take the remaining list and ask the question again. That project is your number two priority. Keep doing this until the list is prioritised.
10. Now cut the project list i.e. draw a line where supply equals demand. Everything above the line can be done. Everything below the line can't be done. And just let's repeat that. *Everything below the line can't be done.* They can't be done because there are no people to do them. Simple as that. And no amount of wishing it were otherwise or sucking it up or saying 'JFDI' or anything else is going to make it otherwise.

HOW YOU NEED TO DO IT
Keeping It Going

1. Plan each of the projects as described in Chapters 1-4 and secure agreement with the stakeholders as in Chapter 5.
2. Begin executing the projects, tracking and reporting them individually as described in Chapter 6.
3. If a new project comes along, don't just launch into it. Rather find a place for it on the prioritised list of projects and make the cut again.
4. To report on summary status of all the projects, score each project according to the following scheme:
   ▶ You have a plan and are running to the plan (green) = 5.
   ▶ You have a plan, have drifted a bit but you're taking steps to fix it (amber) = 3.
   ▶ The project has no written plan (blue) = 0.
   ▶ The project is off the rails (red) = −1.

Add up the scores and divide by the total number of projects. You will get a number between -1 and 5. The closer your number is to 5, the better shape your projects are in; the closer your number is to -1 the worse shape they are in.

WHO YOU NEED TO KNOW
Winston Churchill

All project managers need to have a vision of where they are taking the team and few were more visionary than Winston Churchill, Britain's Prime Minister during the Second World War. In 1938, before the war had even broken out and Neville Chamberlain was trying to appease Hitler, Churchill prophetically said to Chamberlain in the House of Commons, 'You were given the choice between war and dishonour. You chose dishonour, and you will have war'.

When France and the Low Countries were overrun in May 1940, Britain stood alone against Nazi Germany. While there was a certain amount of public sentiment and political opinion in favour of a negotiated peace with Hitler, Churchill was clear in his view that there could be no peace with such a criminal regime. From those dark days in 1940, Churchill united the nation behind him and led it to victory.

A clear vision and outstanding motivation of the team – two of the key requisites for a great project manager.

219

CAREERS IN PROJECT MANAGEMENT

There was a time when the route into project management was a fairly standard one. You went into some technological type industry like construction, information technology or pharmaceuticals, served in some technical capacity for a few years, became some sort of team leader and eventually were promoted to project manager. Often the promotion to project manager was because you couldn't stay technical and get bigger salary increases, so they moved you into management. If you were lucky they'd give you some kind of training course – most of them weren't all that good – and then you were expected to be able to do the business.

Some people did – often by getting scars on their backs. Some people had a natural bent for it and prospered while some people never got the hang of it at all. Almost always the environment was one where impossible missions were the norm.

As we go into the second decade of the 21st century, some things have changed. For starters, it seems like almost everybody these days is running projects. In charities, sporting organisations, not-for-profits, state and semi-state organisations and private companies, people are being handed assignments and being told, 'you're going to be the project manager for this'.

If you find yourself in this situation, be careful. There seems to be a widespread belief in the world that people should naturally know how to manage projects. Perhaps this would be true if we taught it in schools. Every child in the world, right from the time they start school, has to do projects, yet they are never shown how to plan them, estimate them or execute the plans. Imagine that we educated people to be engineers or scientists or accountants but never taught them arithmetic! Perhaps the number of failed projects in the adult world has a lot to do with the fact that children are never taught what is a fundamental, basic skill.

So – there is no reason in the world why you should instinctively know how to manage projects. So if you suddenly find yourself made into a project manager, you need to get the skills quickly.

On the plus side, this means that there are all sorts of routes into project management these days. So if you want to have a career in project management, you can start almost anywhere – indeed, right where you are. What you need then – to become good and respected at your profession are a few things.

First, you need the principles of good project management. You have those already from this book. The first six chapters told you how to run any project successfully.

Second, you need to learn the skill of declining impossible missions i.e. you need to learn negotiating using the facts as described in Chapter 5. Only this way can you be sure that you will become a project manager who always delivers on his/her commitments.

Finally, it would be good to get some professional qualification. Get a PRINCE2 qualification if you're going to be working in environments where this is in use. Become a PMP – Project Management Professional. This is the certification offered by the PMI, the world's number one organisation for project managers. With these three things under your belt, you'll be ready to run any project in any industry anywhere.

WHAT MAKES A GOOD PROJECT MANAGER?

Maybe your team *would* follow you through the fires of hell and out the other side and if so, well done on that. But that isn't necessarily what would make you a good project manager. Here are the things that would – in no particular order:

> ▶ The ability to formulate the goal in a clear and inspiring way – Winston Churchill had it, Abraham Lincoln had it.

► Good at attention to detail – The devil *is* in the detail. You need to care about detail when estimating and when tracking the project.

► Good at communicating – Never forget that a successful project is about happy stakeholders. Identify them, understand what they want, make honest promises to them, stop them from doing harm to themselves by committing to impossible things and keep them in the loop over the life of the project. They'll love you for it.

► You care about and protect your team. In particular you do this by not committing them to sucking it up, to impossible missions, to working burnout hours.

If you have these four things, you'll go a long way.

WHAT YOU NEED TO READ

► The Project Smart website (*www.projectsmart. co.uk*) has plenty of good stuff on the subject of running multiple projects.

► The Office of Government Commerce (OGC) has lots of useful information on projects and programmes on their website at *www.ogc. gov.uk*.

▶ If you need to set up a programme office, *The Program Management Office Advantage* by Lia Tjahjana, Paul Dwyer and Mohsin Habib (Amacom, 2009) has lots that will help you.

▶ *The Soul of a New Machine* by Tracy Kidder (Random House, 1998) was an unlikely best-seller at the time and rightly so. This story of how a group of engineers at Data General set out to design and build a new 32-bit mini-computer in a year is a compelling read.

IF YOU ONLY REMEMBER ONE THING

There has to be enough supply to match the demand. There have to be people to do all the work. Make sure that it's so on your projects.

CHAPTER 8

HAVING A LIFE

WHAT IT'S ALL ABOUT

- ► Why it's okay to have a life
- ► Why better time management is not the answer
- ► Extreme time management
- ► The secret to having a life – the three filters
- ► Saying 'no' nicely
- ► Prioritising viciously
- ► The skill of planning

WHY IT'S OKAY TO HAVE A LIFE

For some bizarre reason, many people – especially bosses and stakeholders – expect project managers to work all the hours God sends. Sometimes project managers accept this as just a normal hazard of the job. There are management-sounding phrases to make the whole business sound respectable. 'Working burnout hours', people say. Or project managers are told to 'sweat their resources'. Or projects are categorised as 'death march projects'.

None of this is normal, of course. Working burnout hours is a terrible idea for a number of reasons.

Let's be clear before we proceed. This is not about a short 'push' to hit a deadline or make a milestone or solve a customer problem. This is about overtime (10–16 hour days) over long, sustained periods of time.

Burnout hours are bad, first and foremost, because they quickly become less efficient than if you had just worked a normal forty hour week. While this may sound counterintuitive, if you think about it you can see why this would be the case.

Imagine, first of all, that you were going to have the hottest date of your life at 8 p.m. this evening. How would you organise your day? Well, to begin with, you'd probably plan to leave at say 5 p.m.. For you this would be a hard deadline every bit as vital as having to catch a plane, a train or pick up kids from the crèche. Just to be on the safe side, you might actually plan to have all your work done by 4 p.m. Then, if some genius did come in to you late in the day looking for something urgent, you would have an hour's contingency to deal with it.

You would plan your day carefully, figuring out exactly what had to get done so that you could leave by 4 p.m. You would be brisk with time wasters, not allowing them to take much of your time and in the process jeopardising your date. The result would be that the important things would get done and you would be ready by 4 p.m. to go home, scrub up, put your glad rags on to get to your rendezvous.

Now contrast this with if you're coming in to face a day which will last from say 8 a.m. to 8 p.m. or later. And this is not an isolated day. You have been doing this for a long time and, as far as you can tell, will continue to do it for the foreseeable future. Not only that, but you haven't been having weekends or evenings to recover from these days. And maybe you haven't been eating or sleeping very well. Or getting much or any exercise. And you haven't been seeing too much of your loved ones. In short, your life has narrowed to being at work, thinking about work, bringing work home with you, or cancelling other things so you can work.

Now how will you spend your day? Well, you will be lazy with your time. Somebody wants to stop for a chat, you'll be happy to chat with them for ages. You may take long breaks or spend time messing around with your inbox or doing any number of other time-wasting things. This is because you know you have a vast amount of hours to spend each day and that if something doesn't get done today then there's always an equally vast number of hours tomorrow. In short – productivity goes out the window.

So – from your management's point of view – the most important reason that working burnout hours is bad is that it's just not productive. There is lots of attendance but not much achievement – at least not as much as there would be if you were just going home on time.

But there are other reasons why working burnout hours is bad and – from your point of view – these are the most important.

Your health suffers – both physical and mental. I both know of and have heard numerous stories of people who have suffered breakdowns through overwork on projects. Your physical health suffers if you don't get a chance to exercise your body properly – and remember, if your body goes, what else is there?

And finally, your relationships suffer. With wives, husbands, partners, girlfriends, boyfriends, children, parents, siblings. I know of marriages that have broken up because of this issue. Or (especially) men wondering where their children's childhoods went.

This situation of work/life balance had become a major issue during the boom years of the late nineties and early noughties. Since the banking crisis, the issue of work/life balance has become even more serious for two reasons. Firstly, organisations have down-sized so that people are having 'to do more with less' as they are constantly told. Not only that, people are also being told that they're 'lucky to have a job'. And having a work/life balance, which was such a hot topic only a couple of years ago, is gone now. You rarely hear people mention it.

At the risk of stating the obvious, all of this is BAD. Furthermore it's possible to do something about it. It's possible not just to tinker with but to solve this problem. But a problem of this severity requires severe medicine to cure it. If you're ready to take the medicine, then read on.

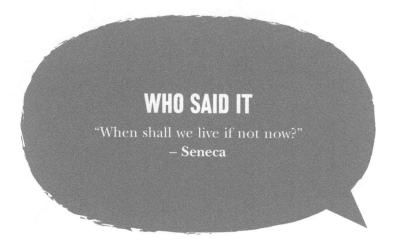

WHO SAID IT

"When shall we live if not now?"
– Seneca

WHO YOU NEED TO KNOW
Mary Davis

During the years leading up to and including 2003 Mary Davis led the team which planned and executed the Special Olympics World Games. Over 7000 athletes plus 3000 coaches and officials came from some 150 countries, and competed in 21 different sports. They were hosted beforehand in 177 communities all over Ireland, North and South. Most of the cost of staging the Games was secured through fund-raising. Mary Davis led a team of 170 people plus many times that number of volunteers to make the Games happen. The Special Olympics World Games was the world's biggest sporting event that year.

In recognising Mary Davis, we are really recognising all of the usually unsung project managers around the world who don't preside over project disasters but rather over huge project successes.

WHY BETTER TIME MANAGEMENT IS NOT THE ANSWER

So is this just a time management problem? Get yourself a book on time management or go on a course and your problem will be solved. Well, you may have done exactly that and you may have found that it helped things a bit, but that it didn't solve the problem.

And it won't. Because time management books or courses don't solve the right problem and the following is the reason why.

Here's a way that you could think about or model the world. In any period of time – the rest of today or the rest of this week or this month or this year or even your whole life – there are a bunch of things that you will have to do – your job, the weekly shopping, mow the lawn, etc. Think of them as a physical pile of stuff, like a pile of bricks. Now place on top of that pile another pile of stuff. These are the things which, in the same period of time, you like to do and would like to do more of. Your hobbies or hanging out with your children or loved one, for example. Next, place on top of that pile another pile of stuff. These are things you hate to do but you have to do them anyway. Paying your taxes, queuing at airports, being stuck in traffic and so on. Finally, place on top of the pile a fourth pile of stuff. These are the things that you were put on earth to do. These are the things which, if you didn't have to bother with the wearisome task of earning a living, you would be doing all the time. These are the things which, if you won the lottery, you would do. Learn to paint or become a rock guitarist or sail around the world or whatever. So there we have it – a great big pile of stuff towering up to the sky.

Now imagine a second pile of stuff. These are the things which in the same period of time - the rest of today or the rest of this week or this month or this year or even your whole life – you will actually do.

In general, for most people, the first pile of stuff is many many times higher than the second pile. Perhaps it has to do with how ambitious you are, or how driven you are. Perhaps it has to do with your age, where you reach a certain point in your life and you start to realise that life isn't infinite after all and that if there are things you want to achieve in your life, you better start thinking of doing them now.

What will going on a time management course or reading a time management book do for you? Well, unless it's a particularly awful course or book, it will have the effect of increasing the second pile. You will become more efficient. You will be able to get more stuff done.

But time management won't solve the problem that the first pile will still be many many times higher than the second pile. This is the problem with time management. It doesn't solve the right problem. It implies that it will but it doesn't really. And this is not to rubbish time management. It has its place and does good things. But it doesn't solve the problem you need to solve. For that you need more radical medicine.

WHO SAID IT

"One of the symptoms of an approaching nervous breakdown is the belief that one's work is terribly important."
– Bertrand Russell

EXTREME TIME MANAGEMENT

Is there a solution to the problem that is described above? Well actually, there is. It's the simple one, the obvious one and – for most people – a terrifying one. The solution to the problem of there being much more to do than time available to do it (notice that it's that old business of supply and demand again) is that *you must learn not to do things.* If you can do this then the right stuff will get done. And by 'the right stuff', I mean that unique combination of things from each of the four categories

– have to do/like to do/hate to do but have to do anyway/was born to do – that's right for you.

This is probably the first time anybody has suggested anything like this to you. In fact, if you think about it, right from the time you started school and maybe even earlier, you have been used to exactly the opposite of that. People have told you to do stuff and you have done it.

Remember that first day in school. Somebody gave you bricks or plasticine or a colouring book and told you to do stuff with it. And being the well-balanced child that you were, you did. Then on through primary school and secondary school, you got assignments, homework, projects, continuous assessment, people getting you to do stuff. If you did some kind of third level education, the same thing. End of term papers, projects, dissertations, theses. And maybe you had part-time jobs while you were in school or college and people told you to do stuff there and you did. And then you began your first 'real' job and what did you get? Job descriptions, objectives, key results areas – always people telling you to do stuff. And basically – right up to the day they're going to haul you out feet first – that's probably the way you saw it being. People would be telling you to do stuff and you would be responding by saying, 'how can I pack this in to an already overcrowded life?'

But if you can learn the skill of not doing things – and it is a skill, just like using a computer or project management or chairing a meeting - you can not just tinker with this, your own personal supply – demand problem. You can solve it. And wouldn't that be a grand thing? So how do you do that?

THE SECRET TO HAVING A LIFE – THE THREE FILTERS

Picture the following. Your sitting in your seat slumped across your desk. Why are you slumped across your desk? Well, imagine your desk as being inside and at the bottom of, a giant silo or cylinder. What happens then is that people throw stuff in the top of the silo. Let's start at work.

Your boss throws stuff – requests to do things. Your team, colleagues, peers throw stuff. Other departments throw stuff. Moving outside work to home, your wife/husband/girlfriend/boyfriend/partner/flatmates/housemates throw stuff. Your family throws stuff. The community in which you live, the government throw stuff. Other people throw stuff and last of all, you throw stuff yourself. All of this stuff comes raining down on your back. No wonder you're slumped!

But it's possible to have a different picture. Instead of your desk being at the bottom of a silo, think of it as being at the bottom of a funnel. And the funnel has three filters in it. Exactly the same volume of stuff from exactly the same sources gets thrown in the top of the funnel. But this time it's filtered. Some things get stopped by the first filter so that only a smaller number get through. Some things get stopped by the second filter so that only a still smaller number get through. And some things get stopped by the third filter so that only a manageable number get through. You're not slumped any more now. You're sitting up and you've got a smiley face ☺ because now you've got a life. Now the right stuff is being done. Imagine how happy you would be in those circumstances.

So all that remains to do then is to figure out what the filters are and begin to apply them. That's what the rest of this chapter is about.

Filter 1: Learn and Practise The Skill of Saying 'No' Nicely

You have to learn and practise the skill of saying 'no' nicely. To get you started here are just a few ways:

1. As somebody approaches (to ask you to do something) look intently at your computer screen or pick up a piece of paper and stare at it as though it were Einstein's Theory of General Relativity. Then try to speak before

they speak and say, 'Look, I'm really involved in this at the moment. Is there any chance you could come back in an hour?' Pretty much everybody respects it. Nobody takes offence. And guess what? Well sometimes they don't come back. And if the don't come back that's great because it's one less thing being thrown into the hopper that you have to deal with. And sometimes, even if they do come back, they've now got several things they want to talk to you about. (All of us know people who could be described as 'serial interrupters'.)

2. Make a sign and hang it up on your door or cubicle that says, 'Your lack of planning is *not* my emergency'. (As a verbal alternative to this, when they ask you to do something – just when you're about to go home or go off for the weekend – say, 'How long have you known about this?' They will invariably blurt out the answer, not realising what a loaded question it is. Then you have a choice of saying either, 'Tough, I'm outta here' or 'I'm gonna do this for you now but don't ever do this to me again.' Either way – they won't!)

3. Say, 'I can't do that for personal reasons'. (Particularly good when said by women to men.)

4. Implement red time and green time. This is the idea that you divide your day up into red time (can't be disturbed/interrupted) and green time (accepting interruptions). So you

might decide, for example, that from 10–12 and from 2–4 were red times. Then if somebody came to you at 9:59 you would give them time/energy/commitment, all that good stuff, but if somebody came at 10:00, you would ask then to come back at 12:00.

5. Go missing. Sit at somebody else's desk. Go hide in a conference room. Or another floor. Or in another part of the building. Work in the cafeteria or restaurant. Or a nearby coffee shop. Or work from home. Anything which potentially reduces the flow of stuff coming to you is good.

6. When somebody asks you to do something, say, 'I'll do this but then I can't do that. Substitution (like this) is obviously not as good as getting rid of the thing altogether, but at least it stops the pile of stuff going into the hopper from getting any bigger.

7. Take a ticket. Say, 'could you send me an email on that?' How many times have you been faced with somebody working out the problem in real time, right before your eyes, wasting *your* time? Let them use their own time. Notice that the idea of take a ticket / write me an email is what support desks do all the time. Guess what? Sometimes people couldn't be bothered and hey presto – the thing goes away.

8. Say, 'I don't have time to look at that right now.'

9. Say, 'Charlie would be a better guy to do that.'

10. Say no to impossible missions as described in Chapter 5. This can stop many of your problems at source.

11. Never say 'yes' or 'sure' to anything. Somebody asks you to do something today, ask would it do tomorrow. Always question the deadline they have given you. We have all had the experience of busting our butt to do something and then they say, 'There was no rush. It would have done next week'.

12. Just say, 'no thanks'. It's the simplest way there is of saying no nicely.

And these are just a handful of ways. If you were given the task of coming up with say, ten more ways of saying no nicely, five that you could use in work and five at home, then it would probably take you no more than ten minutes. (And just while we're on the subject, the idea of saying no nicely is applicable in your personal life as well).

Not all of these will work in all situations with everybody. Different ones will work with different personalities. The point is that it's possible to say no politely without harming your relationship with the other person. Saying no nicely is also the first basic skill you have to learn if you're to become good at not doing things. If you can't master this, then the rest isn't going to work for you.

This section begins with the words 'learn and practise'. Now that you've learned a few how will you practise them?

239

HOW YOU NEED TO DO IT
Saying No Nicely

1. Come up with ten *more* ways of saying no nicely, five that you could use at home and five in work.
2. Now you have a list of more than twenty ways of saying no nicely.
3. Begin to try them out. Say no nicely for a whole day. Or if that sounds hopelessly optimistic, do it for half a day. (Red time and green time would do that for you.) Or if *that* sounds too optimistic, do it for an hour. And then a couple of hours. And then a half a day and then a day. Practice the skill – because it is only a skill. Get good at it. Make a game out of it – say no nicely every second time, for example.
4. Set a target for saying no nicely – 'I'm going to say no nicely on Monday, Wednesday and Friday', for example – and reward yourself if you achieve it.
5. You will know you're getting good at this skill if, when somebody asks you to do something, your instinctive reaction is not, 'how can I fit this in to an already overcrowded life?' but rather, 'how can I wriggle out of this?'

WHO SAID IT

"Being busy does not always mean real work. The object of all work is production or accomplishment and to either of these ends there must be forethought, system, planning, intelligence, and honest purpose, as well as perspiration. Seeming to do is not doing."
— **Thomas Edison**

Filter 2: Learn and Practice The Skill of Prioritising Viciously

Clearly, you can't and don't want to say 'no' to everything. Some things from each of your four categories have to be done. Indeed some of them you will very much want to do. How you decide what those are is what the second filter is all about.

Before explaining prioritising viciously, remember (from the last chapter) what prioritising is. Prioritising is the idea of 'if I could only do one thing what would it be?' Prioritising viciously takes this a stage further. Having prioritised your list using the if-I-could-only-do-one-thing method, you then cut the list where supply equals demand. Everything above the cut you give it time, energy, commitment, the best of everything you have to offer. Everything below the cut you say no nicely to it. Let it go. Cut it loose. Ignore it. Forget about it.

Here's another way to think about all this. Some things are WILDLY important – and many things ... well, just aren't. So, if you can identify the things that really matter – whether in your work or in your life – then lots of stuff just drops away. This is the skill of prioritising viciously. Having learnt it, you need to practise it. How to do that is described in the next section.

WHO SAID IT

"The mass of men lead lives of quiet desperation and go to the grave with the song still in them."
– Henry David Thoreau

HOW YOU NEED TO DO IT
Prioritising Viciously

1. Do a Dance Card list exactly as we described in Chapter 3. (You can do one for your private life in exactly the same way.)
2. Prioritise the list using the if-I-could-only-do-one-thing method.
3. Now prioritise the list viciously – identify what's WILDLY important
4. You will almost certainly have to agree this with your boss and maybe other stakeholders – so go do that.
5. Make sure that the things you have identified as being wildly important are boxes not clouds (remember back to Chapter 1). The things you have identified as being wildly important – your objectives – need to be crystal clear, so that there will be no doubt in anybody's mind that they have been achieved. Lots of people end up with objectives like 'keep the customers happy' or 'get the projects done on time' or 'make the world a better place for little furry animals'. These are no good. Your objectives need to be SMART (Specific, Measurable, Achievable, Realistic, Time-bound) as described in Chapter 1. Go

talk to your boss and have the conversation that begins, 'Hey boss, when the end of the year comes, how would we both know that I've done an *amazing* job?' All objectives can be made SMART. Some, like a sales target, for example, are easy to do. Others take a bit more teasing out. But they can all be done.

6. Now that you have identified what is wildly important and what isn't, live it. That is to say, when something comes in that is wildly important, give it your best. When something comes in that isn't, ignore it by saying no nicely to it.

7. Be prepared to keep testing whether those things that you've identified as wildly important, really are. For example, if there's a regular meeting you go to and you're not convinced of the value of it, then try not going and see what happens. Say you can't make it this week because you've got something else that's a higher priority. Or ask if you can do your bit first and then leave. Or say, 'call me if you need me'. Would the meeting go on if you were sick or (heaven forbid) dead? Probably. Maybe it doesn't matter that much. Or maybe it does – but be prepared to test information.

Filter 3: Learn and Practice the Skill Of Planning

Finally then, for the things that have to be done you want to make sure that they get done with the least amount of effort and fire fighting. But of course you already know how to do this because you know that a little planning is better than a lot of fire fighting.

So in summary then, you can see how the funnel and the filters work. Some things don't get done at all. The things that get done are the things that correspond to your objectives – whether in work or in life. Those things that have to get done, get done with the least amount of effort.

And how do you do planning? Hey – you know all about it. It's in the first five chapters of this book.

WHAT YOU NEED TO READ

▶ Both the Time Management Guide (*www.time-management-guide.com*) and Time Thoughts (*www.timethoughts.com*) contain useful information on the subject of time management.

▶ If you do insist on undertaking impossible missions, then you will probably find some useful ideas in *Death March* by Edward Yourdon (Prentice Hall, 2003). But it is far better not to undertake them in the first place.

▶ If you're looking for a book on time management, David Allen's *Getting Things Done* (Piatkus Books, 2002) is a good place to start.

▶ Tom DeMarco always has plenty of wise things to say and *Slack: Getting Past Burn-out, Busywork, and the Myth of Total Efficiency* (Dorset House, 2001) gives you plenty of those.

IF YOU ONLY REMEMBER ONE THING

Learn the skill of saying no nicely – it is a mandatory skill in business and in life - and you should become good at it.

ACKNOWLEDGEMENTS

Thank you to Ellen Hallsworth at Wiley for giving me the opportunity to write this book.

This was the second project I've done with Jenny Ng at Wiley and, if anything, this was an even bigger pleasure than the first time out. Jenny is the best of co-pilots and any author lucky enough to work with her, should count themselves fortunate indeed.

And finally thank you to Darin Jewell, my tireless and immensely competent agent.

INDEX

Lightning Source UK Ltd.
Milton Keynes UK
UKHW02f2132131018
330485UK00002B/4/P

9 780857 081315